Quiet Dangers

Quiet Dangers

Navigating the Psychological Challenges of Spiritual Intimacy

Robert J. Wicks

Paulist Press
New York / Mahwah, NJ

Cover image by Alex Izeman / Shutterstock.com
Cover and book design by Lynn Else

Library of Congress Cataloging-in-Publication Data
Wicks, Robert J, author.
Title: Quiet dangers : navigating the psychological challenges of spiritual intimacy: "soulful, inspiring, and practical" / Robert J. Wicks.
Description: New York / Mahwah, NJ : Paulist Press, [2023] | Includes bibliographical references. | Summary: "Dr. Wicks writes about resistance to spiritual growth and change and draws upon well-known contemporary voices to elucidate the journey toward a deeper relationship with the truth about ourselves, others, and God"—Provided by publisher.
Identifiers: LCCN 2022040308 (print) | LCCN 2022040309 (ebook) | ISBN 9780809156504 (paperback) | ISBN 9780809188116 (ebook)
Subjects: LCSH: Christian sociology. | Spirituality—Psychological aspects.
Classification: LCC BT738 .W475 2023 (print) | LCC BT738 (ebook) | DDC 261.8—dc23/eng/20221209
LC record available at https://lccn.loc.gov/2022040308
LC ebook record available at https://lccn.loc.gov/2022040309

ISBN 978-0-8091-5650-4 (paperback)
ISBN 978-0-8091-8811-6 (e-book)

Published by Paulist Press
997 Macarthur Boulevard
Mahwah, New Jersey 07430
www.paulistpress.com

Printed and bound in the
United States of America

For Marie Gipprich
A dear friend whose love is shown
in such quiet ways that I only wish
I could show her a movie of how her
generosity has planted new peace
and joy in so many others' lives.

Advanced Reviews for *Quiet Dangers*

"Often the spiritual and the psychological are separated from one another, with some religious people thinking that they don't need psychology if they have religion; and some secular types thinking they don't need religion since they have psychology. In this soulful, inspiring, and practical new book, Robert Wicks, a trained psychologist and spiritual writer, brings the two disciplines together to reveal how the fully alive, fully human, and fully whole person needs both a healthy psyche and soul."

James Martin
Author, *Learning to Pray*

"One of the most important endeavors one can embark upon in life is the search for truth. Within that journey, the quest for the true self unfolds. It is a journey that involves self-questioning and a healthy dose of spiritual doubt, as Dr. Robert Wicks points out in this engaging and inspiring book. The path to truth is rarely—perhaps never—a straight line, but one with peaks, curves, and downslopes. It necessitates the work of both mind and spirit. Drawing on his extensive experience as a psychologist, as well as the wisdom of a variety of spiritual masters, Dr. Wicks offers us a clear roadmap for recognizing the hidden ways we try to avoid the truth. He sets down as guideposts the spiritual values of honesty, humility, transparency, compassion, commitment, courage, gratefulness, and prayer. As he rightly notes, there is no such thing as a "spiritual graduation," only a pilgrimage that leads through one door, then another and another. This book reassures us that with each step we move closer to love—love of ourselves, love of others, and love of God—and to a life that Rabbi Abraham Heschel describes as deserving of 'an eternal Amen.'"

Judith Valente
Former correspondent for *Religion & Ethics NewsWeekly* on PBS-TV
Author, *How to Live: What the Rule of St. Benedict Teaches Us about Happiness, Meaning, and Community*

"Robert Wicks expertly employs psychology and spirituality to uncover 'hidden rooms' in our personalities. These rooms have the potential to hinder or enhance our identity before God, ourselves, and others. Dr. Wicks presents, among other resources, clear and practical descriptions of therapies which may provide insight and offer paths forward. He also weaves into the text spiritual guidance, encouraging the perennial practices of solitude, silence, and contemplative prayer. Throughout, Wicks sharpens the discussion with insightful quotations from a range of wisdom figures. And he regularly lists helpful ways of engaging the material. This work is instructive and inspiring, rich and layered, and a solid companion for a pilgrim on a journey of faith."

John Welch, OCarm
Author, *An Interior Life: Rummaging through the Christian Tradition*

Advanced Reviews for Quiet Dangers

"Drawing upon his years of experience as a psychologist and spiritual mentor, Robert Wicks combines his personal insights and wide knowledge of wisdom writers in an engaging work that is parable-like in its ability to disempower our resistance to seeing the true patterns of our thinking and behaving. Bringing together practical suggestions with engaging stories in a style that is wisely evocative, Wicks invites us into a safe space where we are challenged to see what we have hidden from ourselves and from God and how our own stories can be rewritten in the language of love and humility."

Thomas E. Rodgerson
Author, *Overhearing a Christian Apology to the Nones: Revealing Still Hidden Truths in Dialogue*

Terms

SPIRITUAL INTIMACY

Openness to a deeper relationship with the truth about yourself, others, and God.

PSYCHOLOGICAL RESISTANCE

The phenomenon in which persons either directly or indirectly, unconsciously or with only partial awareness, oppose facing the truth about themselves, others, or a situation.

METANOIA

A change of heart, conversion, letting go, Repentance; a sadness for the missed transformative moments in life.

Table of Contents

Table of Contents

Acknowledgments

I would like to thank Oxford University Press for permission to adapt material from my books *Perspective: The Calm within the Storm* and *Bounce: Living the Resilient Life* (Second Edition). I would also like to express gratitude to my wife, Michaele Barry Wicks, for her detailed and insightful editorial suggestions.

Prologue

~ Quiet Dangers ~

Confronting Compartmentalization and Other Psychological Defenses against Truth, Openness, and Change

The truth may be puzzling. It may take some work
    to grapple with.
It may be counterintuitive. It may contradict
    deeply held prejudices.
It may not be consonant with what we
    desperately want to be true.
But our preferences do not determine what's
    true.

– Carl Sagan

"Is there anything I can do to make myself enlightened?"

"As little as you can do to make the sun rise in the morning."

"Then of what use are the spiritual exercises you prescribe?"

Quiet Dangers

"To make sure you are not asleep when the sun begins to rise."

– Anthony de Mello
One Minute Wisdom

Sometimes tradition without truth is merely an error with a long history.

– Cyprian of Carthage
Epistle 73

Over thirty years ago, Dutch Catholic priest, professor, and writer Henri Nouwen expressed interest in an idea I had to write a book on navigating the psychological challenges, even perils, of spiritual intimacy. The timing for its development wasn't right until now. However, given the current turmoil in society and religion, delaying it any further at this point would seem wrong. The potent desire to find meaning and centeredness in the truth is needed more today than ever before. The following reflections are offered in response to this longing—not so much to provide answers but to walk with the readers as they uncover and grapple with the questions held in their own hearts that they may have set aside but which now deserve the light of day.

When we are very young, many of us experienced a vibrant faith marked by simplicity. When such simplicity is present, it brings with it a wonderous sense of faith as one participates in religious ritual as well as when experiencing awe when hearing the Word of God in Sacred Scripture. Being small and approaching the creche at Christmas and seeing the size of the little statue of Jesus as a child also helped us to realize that there is nothing to be afraid of in the presence of God...and so we have much in which to rejoice! Encountering a statue of a smiling child who is also God helps us to realize it is not power that is most divine...*it is love*!

Then adolescence dawns and often brings with it a questioning of all things—including both religion and faith. Yet, there is still enough simplicity during this time of life that is joined with the beginnings of maturity to mark the blessings of this phase. As one adolescent said when asked by her father whether she got used to the gorgeous Florida skies after being in university there for a number of years: "I know that the beauty of these skies is for everyone here, but I also feel God painted them *just for me*."

It is also natural for persons at this age to see clearly, be persons without guile, and not easily tolerate hypocrisy—especially in older persons and religious leaders who say one thing and behave differently without being able to explain rationally why they do.

As a result, if adults attend church regularly and say religious words but don't model what they are proclaiming, questions often arise from teenagers:

- "How can you attend church on Sundays and use such foul language?"
- "How can you say you pray and follow the Gospel but still treat people of other races or from other countries as garbage?"
- "They just taught us about the Beatitudes at Sunday school. How can you support politicians who say they are 'right to life' but cage children seeking refuge, are known to treat women only as sexual objects, and close their eyes to those dying at the border or the poor seeking health care?"

Adolescents don't suffer gladly those persons who demonstrate a significant distance between their stated religious ideals and daily actions. I think cartoonists on the Op-Ed pages of newspapers must be adolescents at heart because their minds and art cut right to the core. In this spirit, Australian critic, journalist, and broadcaster Clive James once referred to cartoons as "cultural shorthand." And so, I wasn't surprised when during the 2020 U.S. presidential campaign, while children were caged and dying at the border, I saw a cartoon portraying a golden statue of one of the candidates holding up a Bible while a group of Christians were bowing before him. When the emperor has no clothes both teenagers and cartoonists can point out quite vividly hypocrisy. As theologian and mystic Karl Rahner once noted, "The number one cause of atheism is Christians. Those who proclaim Him with their mouths and deny Him with their actions is what an unbelieving world finds unbelievable." Or, in the words of well-known theologian, philosopher, and writer Abraham Joshua Heschel in his book *God in Search of Man*:

> It is customary to blame secular science and antireligious philosophy for the eclipse of religion in modern society. It would be more honest to blame religion for its own defeats. Religion declined not because it was refuted, but because it became irrelevant, dull, oppressive, insipid. When faith is completely replaced by creed, worship by discipline, love by habit; when the crisis of today is ignored because of the splendor of the past; when faith becomes an heirloom rather than a living fountain; when religion speaks only in the name of authority rather than with the voice of compassion—its message becomes meaningless.

After the teenage years, adulthood slowly dawns with its own challenges and charms. At this stage, with many levels within it, the calling is to prune adolescence in order to retain its honesty, passion, and simplicity, while eliminating its possible naïveté. Some respond to the callings and demands of this stage with great energy. Still others settle for a vague spiritual sense or even abandon both religion and faith altogether. While others seek to return to childhood to recapture what they remembered as "a simple faith." Since this is impossible, given the complex issues of life which the adult is called to confront, the result is that they run the danger instead of becoming simplistic. This may, in some cases, also result in their becoming "uber religious," which potentially may lead to even more prejudice against anything that might cause them to encounter the confusion, concern, challenges, or deep doubt that naturally comes with mature faith. Their unconscious goal in such behavior is to have enough religion to be comfortable. Yet, they don't have enough *faith* to recognize the challenges and questions arising in seeking God and therefore sadly miss the rewards of true spiritual simplicity and honesty, as well as the inner peace and true joy on the other side of facing such uncertainty.

Adults who behave this way have retired from living with a dynamic God. They would rather avoid entering a messy world even if it means they could actually experience a faith that is alive, vibrant, and *real*. Their real prayer is: "Come, Holy Spirit, so we can tame you." It is not the true spiritual cry "Speak Lord for we as Your servants listen and obey." Instead, it really is: "Listen Lord, so we can speak about the outcomes *we* personally desire."

Through the centuries, spiritual sages have taught us that there are psychological and spiritual roads that may feel comfortable but are not "the narrow path" about which Jesus spoke. Moreover, we need to be cautious and recognize that simply because we can find other believers who get in the same religious spiritual boat with us, that it doesn't also guarantee the boat is going in the right direction! Again, in the words of

Jesus, "But small is the gate and narrow the road that leads to life, and only a few ever find it" (Matt 7:14).

Instead, contemplative, Trappist monk, and spiritual writer Thomas Merton advised that with deep faith comes deep doubt, so we need to give up the business of suppressing doubt. In saying this, he is pointing out that in an ongoing journey toward psychological and spiritual maturity, the search is *not* so much for pat and final answers. Instead, it involves the willingness to be involved in an openness to larger and deeper questions. They may disturb us in the short run. However, such a journey in honesty will eventually open portals to a deeper, more energetic faith needed at different junctures in time *if* we don't run away or make excuses for freezing in place. Jennifer Anna Sosetti-Ferencei in her book *On Being and Becoming* indicates a similar sentiment held by the Danish author, philosopher, and religious thinker, Søren Kierkegaard. She notes that his understanding of the paradox of faith required "both radical uncertainty and passionate commitment."

It is this very type of encounter with the Truth, the Spirit, that we see reflected in Sacred Scripture where we have the opportunity to view a constant dialogue between God and the human race. This is also the case when we are theologically reflecting on the *past*, seeking to involve ourselves in moral reasoning in the *present*, and discerning where God is calling us in the *future*. That is an alive faith!

Adults who embrace life as an ongoing pilgrimage realize there is no final "spiritual graduation." As a matter of fact, to the contrary, there is a need in an adulthood marked by wisdom, more than at any other stage of development, to recognize and embrace the one constant in life: *change*. As poet and essayist Kathleen Norris points out in her book *Dakota*, "When we turn our back on change, we don't recapture the past. We lose the future."

Such a mature knowledge of life is, once again, not evidenced by having all the answers...but instead by having a spirit of *humility*. The reason for this is that when we take knowledge and add humility, we get true wisdom. And, when we take that very wisdom and add it to a life of compassion and meaning, we get love...and *God is love*.

And so, navigating the psychological challenges or perils of spiritual intimacy is not tantamount to being able to circumvent or conquer the challenges of life—that is mere religious fantasy. Instead, it is a willingness to enter the darkness *fully*, being willing to question our own self-image and our sense of who God is, and to directly face the doubts, questions, needs, stresses, anxieties, and sadness that arise in any committed life. It is to face *all* of our life clearly, completely, and honestly, *without leaving anything out*.

Introduction

~ Rooms Hidden from God ~

In a piece written on the theme of "humility," Anthony de Mello, in his collection of brief dialogues entitled *One Minute Wisdom*, shared the following interaction:

> To a visitor who described himself as a seeker after Truth the Master said, "If what you seek is Truth there is one thing you must have above all else."
>
> "I know. An overwhelming passion for it."
>
> "No. An unremitting readiness to admit you may be wrong."

Or, to quote Rabbi Heschel again, "We are closer to God when we are asking questions than when we think we have answers."

There is a psychological defense mechanism designed to prevent finding the whole truth about something or about yourself for that matter. It is called "compartmentalization." Its purpose is to separate conflicting values, ideas, beliefs, cognitions (ways of thinking, understanding, and perceiving), and activities in order to avoid seeing an uncomfortable truth about yourself and life. By mentally breaking up and separating such opposing philosophies or ways of living, they are able to exist side by side without causing any anxiety. It is an extreme form of rationalization in which the person seals off a style of thinking and behaving so as to avoid feelings of guilt and anxiety. Often it is done with the agreement of others who are employing the same defense.

Such use of compartmentalization can be minor or major, personal or systemic in nature. Since it is an unconscious defense against fully embracing the truth, the person has no complete awareness of it. Consequently, if a person or organization is challenged as to its use, walls of denial and rationalization are employed because there is no awareness that the defense is in place. And so, when confronted, they logically respond with such dismissive comments as the following:

- "You don't understand the *total* situation."
- "If only you knew why I was doing it."
- "It's only to protect the institution (church, religiously founded health care, or educational system) and help it succeed."
- "Never question my integrity!"

Rabbi Abraham Joshua Heschel offered a beautiful biblical image for this. He said that when Adam and Eve were thrown out of the Garden of Eden, they simply reacted by creating their own garden and then threw God out. With the unconscious defense of compartmentalization, whether individually, with the assistance of a like-minded group, or with an enabling structure of administration without the presence of a prophetic voice, a structure is created to avoid cognitive dissonance (the mental state of having inconsistent thoughts, beliefs, or attitudes, especially as relating to behavioral decisions and attitude change). The result can cause significant psychological and spiritual harm to the person using it, the institution, or persons in the interpersonal network in which it is being employed.

The most dramatic examples of the use of compartmentalization became evident when the sexual, physical, religious, and spiritual abuse of individuals came to light in organized religion. In many cases the persons involved in such abuse were quite conservative in their beliefs, emphasized the need to be meticulous in religious rituals, and were quite strict in the advice or supervision they offered others. This was being done all during the time when they were quietly sexually abusing children or spiritually abusing those who came to them for help. Physical abuse was also a factor in such places as homes for unwed mothers where women were seen as children not fit to offer home environments in which to raise children themselves. The fact that compartmentalization worked to keep the abusers from being anxious or contrite points to the significant hidden negative power of this *unconscious* defense against seeing what they were doing as wrong.

Systemic Compartmentalization—Examples of "Unconscious Arrogance"

Systemically, the defense of compartmentalization also shows itself even when it doesn't involve sexual, physical, or spiritual abuse. In such cases when this occurs, it is dangerous to the spirit and charism of the organization in which it takes place. For instance, in a health care setting a female or male religious ("Sister," "Brother," or Priest) is in the cafeteria giving a talk on the founder or foundress of their religious order to new employees, while the CEO and CFO are up in the corporate headquarters making financial decisions that have moral implications in terms of service to the poor and marginalized. When this happens the separation of power from ethical and spiritual values is obvious.

In religiously based educational institutions, the lines are more vaguely drawn and quietly enacted, so the dangers are even greater. In working with presidents in such colleges and universities, a number of questions can be posed to prevent systemic compartmentalization:

> *How often have you consulted current as well as former and retired chairpersons as you plan to make major changes in their departments? After all, don't they, or haven't they, filled one of the most difficult positions in the university: middle managers? In many cases, haven't they given many, many years of their professional life to your institution because they believed and worked hard to support its mission?*
>
> *Do you believe that consulting others who may not agree with you is an excellent way to uncover immature or unconscious reasons to eliminate or change programs or missions?*
>
> *Since there are numerous secular universities, how does this decision support the charism of your school and not simply reflect a desire for respect or your own—albeit unconscious—willfulness?*

We already have plenty of public hospitals and universities. If a hospital founded by a religious organization is not concerned about providing health care for the poor, why should it exist? If a university established by a religious group makes decisions regarding programs and policies without collaboration, or consultation, with existing and former leaders who have been managers and stewards of the *charism* of the school—especially in areas that are spiritually oriented—where is the sense of tapping into corporate wisdom as a key part of spiritual discernment? This is even the case when we simultaneously honor the realm of ultimate decision-making power that leaders should be able to exercise since they are privy to "the big picture."

The Jesuits (members of the Society of Jesus) have a wonderful and apt saying with respect to this that honors discernment, the chain of command, and being obedient. It is: "We discern...he decides." This is in reference to members working with their spiritual director regarding a change in ministry that appreciates that no matter what they come up with, the provincial still has the final word. However, a religious mission is in danger of being compromised or secularized when there is limited consultation and collaboration by provincials, CEOs of religiously founded health care institutions, presidents of educational institutions that have a religious affiliation, or bishops of dioceses. As one priest told me, "Our bishop feels he has consulted with the priest when he tells the priest about his reassignment a couple of weeks ahead of time."

Compartmentalization—personal and systemic—is a powerful, quiet defense that operates among us all. We not only see it in religious leaders but encounter it in *all of us* as well, since it can be seen both as personal and systemic in nature. The key is being willing to be truly open enough to find those areas where we may be wrong in our decisions.

This defense shows up in ways that can be so destructive, especially among those who have visibly dedicated themselves to God. Once, when a pastor was asked about the rigidity and immaturity of a young man causing hurt to his peers in his youth group while simultaneously thinking about entering the seminary, the pastor responded, "He is like his mother in that regard. She comes to church faithfully but would have no remorse about verbally offering cutting remarks to someone in the parish who doesn't agree with her religious tenets."

Being open to hearing a prophetic voice is essential if compartmentalization is to be unveiled for what it is doing destructively to others...*and ourselves.* No one likes to hear the voice of a prophet. Possibly author and naturalist, Henry David Thoreau was thinking of such a person when he once said, "If you see someone coming to do good for you, run for your life." Or, similarly, in the poetic words of holocaust survivor and author, Elie Wiesel, when he said in the colorful, powerful way he was known for: "When you see an angel of the Lord coming with the words, 'Be not afraid,' you know you are in trouble." However, it is important to have prophetic voices as well as those who are willing to recognize past errors in one's interpersonal network and system/organization. As the late Archbishop Desmond Tutu noted, "We realized how much we had denied ourselves until 1992. Now we have the first two Anglican women bishops on the African continent, and we are asking ourselves why we were so stupid for so long."

Another aid in seeking the truth is the simple process of contemplation where we spend time alone with God to hear the Divine voice. Still, even this is insufficient in and of itself because many of us fall for the temptation to be alone with our own ego and listen to our own views, rather than truly open ourselves to real contemplation. One seminary rector said to me that one of his students was very divisive and judgmental. In response I asked, "Well, does he meditate in silence, solitude, and wrapped in gratitude before God?" The response was, "Yes, he sits before the Blessed Sacrament faithfully but then comes out of the chapel and immediately gossips about the other seminarians and faculty."

Thomas Merton once noted his appreciation for the Abbas (fathers) and Ammas (mothers) of the desert. He said they flocked to barren areas after the church was declared no longer an outlaw religion by Constantine. They feared the domestication of their faith. However, not all went to the desert to be with God. Some simply went to be dramatically by themselves, and they went crazy.

Fortunately, or maybe in extreme cases *unfortunately*, most persons who employ the unconscious defense mechanism of compartmentalization, don't go crazy. Instead, they and we—when using this psychological defense—operate "sanely" and surely, professing to be following God, while not being really faithful to mission beyond the "holy" words we utter, the pietistical emails we send out, or the lectures or homilies we deliver that contain broad religious sentiments. However, if one's circle of friends includes the "prophet" who challenges us appropriately to appreciate our resistance to experiencing true contemplation, we would see when are behaving pridefully like the emperor who didn't wear clothes. Then we could deal with issues clearly, kindly, and prayerfully. When we don't navigate the psychological perils of spiritual intimacy, the road may seem easier for us to travel, but the ultimate negative results eventually become painfully clear.

Several years ago, there were accounts written and published by two nuns who had been sexually abused early in life. One account was very "rosy." You could tell she had decided to use religion and pious language to psychologically paper over or religiously circumvent what she faced. It was a clear case of "spiritual romanticism." She was using religion as a "spiritual cortisone," as a way to hide her questions, trauma, fears, doubts, and pain.

The other account detailed a nun railing at God and questioning where the Lord was when she was abused and most needed divine presence. Such honesty in her relationship with God eventually led her to a new, even deeper, and much, much more mature sense of God than she paradoxically could ever have experienced had she not *had an encounter with trauma in the first place*. This is referred to in psychology as "post traumatic growth (PTG)." In religion this has long been seen as "the spirituality of suffering."

Although many of us fortunately won't have to traverse such deep darkness in our own lives as these abused women sadly did, the lesson and paradigm is still there for all of us no matter what levels of darkness we must encounter throughout life. In essence, navigating the psychological perils of spiritual intimacy is well worth the journey in meeting God. As a matter of fact, it is really, in the end, the *only* adult spiritual pilgrimage toward greater intimacy with ultimate meaning and toward experiencing the deepest love possible. *It is life in its fullness*! It is when theonomy (God's will) and autonomy (our will) truly intersect.

True conversion, a repentance and letting go of all that is blocking us from experiencing the truth, God, and our lives fully, is what *Quiet Dangers* is all about. The goal of the following pages is to initiate a richer discussion at the very time when so many givens in both religion and life are being questioned. In a positive, yet realistic, sense, the aim is not to turn away from uncertainty in the world and religion. The response instead must be to face uncertainty in a way that results in a deeper faith and a greater commitment to becoming compassionate in ways that naturally flow from the peace and joy experienced as a result of embracing the life we are being called to live.

And so, this book, once again, is not designed to offer psychological Band-Aids or spiritual remedies. Instead, it is about highlighting the human tendencies during life's challenges to run away when this is not necessary. It is also concerned with psychologically clearing the way so that we come to know what each of us can do on our own, as well as to humbly know there is also darkness that only God can give light to in prayer and spiritual epiphanies.

The Gift of Psychology

Psychology is a gift from God. It is a bit like a "mental shovel" to loosen our inner soil so a new spiritual tree of life and compassion can be planted. Yet, some misjudge or even fear psychology. And so, they stand with "the shovel" in hand and look up to the sky and ask God to dig the hole for them. All of us were given the shovel by God…now we need to use it ourselves rather than asking God to do our job.

Others believe the opposite. They equate psychology with spirituality and faith. This is, in a word, arrogant. Psychology is a wonderful gift for us to use, but it is still merely a gift to enrich our spirituality. Psychology can never match the depth and breadth of faith.

In the end, those who use the gift of psychology to see how they are unconsciously moving toward or away from God experience and share love more freely and deeply. They see when they are worshipping elements of the church and not God. They find out more quickly when they are using religion, religious practice, or Sacred Scripture, not as a way to experience a deeper faith but as a crutch so they don't need to face the call to truly love…everyone.

They also see the need to take care of the earth and welcome the stranger as we are called to do. They may upset some church goers, but they recognize following Christ and what he said and did is the real—and only—goal.

Waving the flag of faith, but not really practicing it in your heart, as well as in your action, is more easily uncovered when we use psychology. Domestication of our faith happens less when we have tools to know ourselves and examine our thinking and fears more clearly.

And even when we hang a cross on a wall in our room, it is done to remind us of the call to walk with God through the darkness, not evidence that we are religious and our job is done. After all, when family and friends come to visit us, they will not simply look at our religious signs and believe. Instead, they will look more intently at us to see if we are living what our mouth and practices proclaim. If our children, friends, and others say, "She is a very religious person" or "He is a faithful church goer" and they don't add: "They are really good souls," then the goals achieved by us are not greater faith but simply religious garb with no substance underneath.

Psychology can help us with modeling what we preach and religiously demonstrate. It is like a helpful shovel so we don't need to use our hands to dig blindly or, worse yet, pray to God to do the work that we should be doing. In pursuit of this, the material to follow is meant simply as a "spiritual commencement address for adults." This is so because only the persons reading what is to follow can take the information offered further in life, in a unique way, following the singular call God has for them. Therefore, in this pursuit, what is to follow is not designed to alleviate responsibility but actually to *heighten* it as we discern and take personal action on what is in our human hands and better recognize and honor what is only in God's power. In the words, once again, of Rabbi Abraham Heschel: "What is the meaning of my being?...What I look for is not how to gain a firm hold on myself and on life, but primarily how to live a life that would deserve and evoke an eternal Amen."

The good news is that if persons have an interest in this overall goal, then it is a reflection that God's grace is *already* being acted upon, whether what is to follow is helpful or not. Having a sense of serious intrigue about the action of God in the world, and in *ourselves*, is a major step to psychologically walking through the portal God has opened for us with such a desire in order to travel the narrow road on which true peace and joy are experienced. In this journey, comfort, success, and pleasure are seen for what they really are: fun…but no more than that. They can't satisfy the deep human urge that only the Ultimate can offer in terms of real joy and peace.

Given this, the information to follow is meant to serve like "a psychological plow" God has given to us to help us sow and reap the rewards of the spiritual fields of life. Only God's grace provides the "plow" and the "produce." But not to use the gift of psychology in this pursuit is tantamount to turning down one of God's major gifts. On the other hand, forgetting that psychology is a gift from God or thinking it is equal to spirituality would also be a mistake and quite arrogant, really. It is tantamount to becoming a Pelagian, who thinks it is possible to go it alone with only one's intellect and will.

And so, with an attitude marked by trust, intrigue, honesty, humility, compassion, commitment, and prayer, the journey begins anew. When our approach contains such virtues, it is simple. Not easy, *ever*, but simple. The final guidance offered as you reflect on the following themes is: if you feel yourself running into problems, ask yourself if the virtues just mentioned need to be called more to bear in your life because you may be encountering unconscious *resistance*. In encountering them, Richard Rohr reminds us that "in the Gospels, we don't see Jesus getting upset with the sinners. We see Him getting upset only with those who do not think they are sinners." St. Vincent de Paul similarly sums up the situation well in noting that "the most powerful weapon to conquer the devil is humility."

Then, if you still feel lost in encountering the following material, turn to a sage you may know to ask for further guidance. Most of all, remember that difficulty is another call to pray more deeply as well as to think and act more broadly *and boldly*. It may help to remember as well that the search for holiness being asked of us is not simply for ourselves, but also for those around us. The importance of seeking to psychologically uncover, befriend, and move away the blocks in encountering

God and life more dramatically, is a desperately desired societal need now—not simply a personal one. As Kenneth Leech in his classic work, *True Prayer*, states,

> To recognize holiness is to recognize the activity of God in people. More than that, holiness manifests the character, the nature of God....Holiness never points to itself but always beyond itself to God. The saint is essentially someone who communicates and radiates the character of God, his love, his joy, his peace....And the world needs saints, Simone Weil wrote, just as a plague-stricken city needs doctors.

In this spirit, *Quiet Dangers* is not meant simply to be of personal benefit, although it hopefully will be, but of its nature it must turn out to be a gift from God to and through us to the world as well. If it is not, then it isn't truly a change of heart and a letting go...a *metanoia*. It is not the genuine spiritual "good news." But if the journey in truth is real, many surprises are in store—even as we question if such a dramatic unity with, and experience of, God is really possible for us. We need persistence, courage, and, most of all, *passion*.

Using the model of John of the Cross can help in this regard. As Iain Matthew, an expert on the life and work of this mystic, notes in the following passage from his book, *Impact of God*:

> "What prepares the soul to be united with God is: the desire for God." Such faith-desire is the dynamo of John's system. When the goal seems impossibly distant, he does not suggest that we settle for something more manageable. He agrees that it is distant, and says [in the following words] that desire will get us there:

> So the soul must desire with all her desire to come to what in this life lies beyond her mind or the capacity of her heart.
>
> It is here that the sureness of touch, which we saw John display in [his poem] the *Flame*, comes to the fore. He never backs down from his statement of divine generosity. If he anticipates readers shaking their heads ("He's gone too far this time"), there is no hint of a "Yes, you're right, let me rephrase that." There is only a "Please believe me."

In light of this, *Quiet Dangers* offers some initial steps. Furthermore, in addition to reading what is written in the following pages, there is:

- A need for *space* in your day to see what is written on your own heart in reaction to the points being made, and illustrations offered, in the following pages.
- The chance to question what you *feel* about the themes.
- Enough time to reflect on the *thoughts* that come to mind during the reading and to be able to examine how realistic and helpful such thinking and perceptions are.
- A willingness during the day to decide how one is going to *act* on what was learned going forward.

Without such time and space, little of what is understood can be transformed into insight that result in a commitment to be more open, loving, appreciative, and compassionate. As was previously mentioned, what is written here is only meant as a "spiritual commencement exercise"; it is as "simple" and as difficult as that. Yet, the fruits of being willing to navigate the psychological perils involved, in seeking to be responsible and free to respond fully to God, are all worth it when we live with a sense of "*spiritual* existentialism"—being in the now seeking the truth of God.

Spiritual Existentialism

In the final chapter of John's Gospel, we receive a three-fold message that includes the:

- Invitation to be nourished: "Come have breakfast."
- Call to be compassionate: "Feed my lambs, tend my sheep."
- Command to be spiritually radical: "Follow me."

If we do this, we will surely fail at times. There are times when we will miss the mark, want to run away, and maybe even become a false prophet. Because embracing truth is part of this journey and is so uncomfortable, upsetting, and challenging, we may also find it easier to take a different path with others who have similar excuses, rationalizations, and fears of uncertainty and loss of comfort and security. And so, though it is never easy, the journey to God must be taken in both hope and trepidation with others who also want no rooms hidden from God. Together we must do it if we are to be faithful. And being faithful doesn't only impact us, it also results in us joining and forming existential spiritual communities.

With a basic existentialist perspective, Jennifer Anna Gosetti-Ferencei in her book *On Being and Becoming* notes,

> From a human perspective, we inhabit a moment of a human world. We each exist, for example, on this train platform or park bench, here under a reading

> lamp, in this library or bookstore, or wherever one happens to be reading these words. Our moment in place and time belongs of course to a particular culture. While contemporary theorists like to insist on the differences among us—in our languages, customs, religions, ethical values, or ways of life—existentialists constantly refer to what all human beings share in common. For our human condition is such that all of us must be born (in some way or other) in order to arrive in the world. We all must die within a limited life span, at a point of which none of us can be certain. We all have both a beginning which we did not choose and an end which we cannot know. None of us can travel back in time to amend our mistakes, nor can we foresee the future. For an existentialist, these shared facts of the human condition vastly override our differences.

Yet, even though we should, *must* take this journey, such a human view and approach, Gosetti-Ferencei acknowledges, is very difficult at times as well. To indicate this, along with our responsibility, she goes on to reflect on and quote the words of the poet Rainer Maria Rilke:

> In sadness, Rilke thinks, something reaches us from beyond ourselves. This something may be negative and yet it may be something which potentially sustains us. In sharp contrast to the Stoic advice to overcome suffering by adopting an attitude of indifference, Rilke offers a reassuring image of sadness as an intrinsic and natural part of life. He thus writes [from *Letters to a Young Poet*]:
>
>> So, you mustn't be frightened...if a sadness rises in front of you, larger than you have

> ever seen; if an anxiety, like light and cloud-shadows, moves over your hands and over everything you do. You must realize that something is happening in you, that life has not forgotten you, that it holds you in its hand and will not let you fall.

For those of us who are persons of faith, the belief is that "something" is God and the call we are responding to is to become part of the "communion of saints" in living out a life in which I would emphasize again, by way of encouragement, theonomy (God's will) and autonomy (our will) intersect so we can experience true freedom and love.

As part of this search for a life of meaning and compassion, living in freedom from psychological, personal, societal, and even limited "religious" resistances to change and truth, includes key questions. They are both large and particular and may bring us back in time so we can move faithfully forward in a positive direction. For instance, we may ask breathtaking questions like: What was life like when the earth was young, the forests lush, and the flowers growing wildly in every direction in numerous colors? This will bring us back to the spirit of Genesis and help us know our role in healing our earth's climate. Another question might be more specific and personal and cause us to ask ourselves, What was it like when *I* was young and filled with spontaneous bursts of laughter and joy? Why am I not more like that now?

In asking these questions of ourselves, life, and Sacred Scripture, we are moving seemingly paradoxically away from our self-centeredness as a way of finding our true selves. In dropping an overconcern with ourselves, we are opening up to finding ourselves in nature, others, and God in a way that we are *larger* and can both claim and respond to the name God has written on the palm of his hands for us. But this requires that we not seek to take a doctrine of our faith and have it do the work for us. Rather, we need to take psychological steps ourselves to make the inner soil ready to receive the seeds God is planting every day *and* simultaneously become more aware when we are doing things consciously and unconsciously to avoid taking care of our inner spiritual garden.

Thomas Merton, in one of his most well-known quotes, puts it this way:

> Every moment and every event of every person's life on earth plants something in his soul. For just as the wind carries thousands of winged seeds, so each moment brings with it germs of spiritual vitality that come to rest imperceptibly in the minds and wills of [people]. Most of these unnumbered seeds perish and are lost, because [people] are not prepared to receive them: for such seeds as these cannot spring up anywhere except in the *good soil* of freedom, spontaneity, and love.

Honesty, transparency, compassion, openness, genuineness, gratefulness, courage, and a sense of adventure in pursuit of truth and the freedom to live fully as God wishes for us are all good "seeds" for us to nurture. And the primary way to do this is to ultimately embrace love as the soil necessary for this to occur. This is what true religion encourages. In the words of the Dalai Lama, "I would like to point out that the purpose of religion is not to build beautiful churches or temples; it is to cultivate positive human qualities such as tolerance, generosity, and love. When it strays from this goal, even though the persons encouraging it mean well, the results fall short."

For instance, religious rules sometimes present themselves as a way to be principled and faithful. When, in reality, they are often simply disguised attempts to control the living, loving

God. It is amazing what even the most intelligent and moral people will do to avoid the uncertainty, doubt, darkness, and challenges involved in a dynamic spiritual relationship. The sad result of this is that not only do people around them suffer their unconscious religious righteousness, but the persons themselves also miss the fullness of a meaningful life resulting from welcoming epiphanies (sudden moments of revelation and insight) and experiencing a sense of wonder and awe. Truly, we need to "walk by faith, not by sight" (2 Cor 5:7).

In listening to God, and not our own ego, questions may then come up that were never considered before. All of a sudden, we may look at church history, for example, and ask, "Why did people fear the heretics and not those who burned them at the stake?" Henry David Thoreau once said, "Not all who wander are lost." To this I would add, in the spirit of the desert fathers and mothers of the fourth and fifth century, "Seek Jesus's Spirit, not simply what some would have us believe because they feel they have the whole truth and don't recognize the quiet dangers to their own humility and spiritual life."

There is a saying from Australia (and I am paraphrasing Wesley Granberg-Michaelson) that goes: You have a choice as to how you herd cattle. You can build a fence or create a well. Rules are like the fences and may make us feel more secure. The well is the good news of Jesus that is frightening because it is new but more so because it is good.

Once we have a sense of God's love in place, there are many changes in how we view life and faithfulness to Jesus's call. Community is seen as more inclusive. Like little children who don't bother about the differences in skin color, wealth, or background but simply want to spend time having fun together, we, too, find ourselves naturally wanting to be generous and in unity. We also don't worry whether we are liked or effective. We just want to be faithful to what is good.

Once, when I had a book published for physicians and

nurses during the onset of the COVID-19 virus, I received a grant from a friend to send them abroad and to groups in the United States who needed support in their stressful work in health care. One box went to a friend in India. When it didn't get there in the time I thought it would, I emailed the female religious I had sent it to, expressing my worry. In response, she simply said, "Your goodness will not get lost." The same can be said of us all when we seek to be completely open to God, the truth about ourselves, and the call to be faithful.

Finally, when we seek psychologically and spiritually to unlock the rooms we have usually inadvertently and unconsciously hidden from God, wise and faithful friends sometimes hold the key that we need to see where these "rooms" are, why we have created them, and how we might find an appreciation of the love of God necessary to know they are no longer necessary. A wise spiritual companion can also gently help us to recognize the times when humility fails us as we unconsciously seek to be god rather than serve God. In these moments, we need to be challenged with the ancient but often now unspoken question: "*Who told you that you are naked?*" In turn, these words also help us reflect upon those times when we are called to walk with others. And so, the spirit of this book, life, and faith, is meant to be shared. Such collaboration is another preparation to avoid the question that sages through time have said will challenge us after death, if we seek to approach the gates of heaven alone: "*You mean you haven't brought anyone with you?*"

1. "Do You Want to Be Made Whole?"

Healthy Self-Awareness and Spiritual Self-Respect

New spiritual directors and psychotherapists are surprised that those who seek their guidance often resist looking at their talents more than at their personal challenges. An exception, of course, are character disordered persons who manifest "pure projection" in which the problems they are experiencing are never their fault. It is always *others* who are the source of the problem.

This can be seen more readily in some well-known persons from the entertainment and sports industries as well as, most recently, among certain flamboyant politicians and high-profile preachers. However, these individuals rarely seek psychotherapy unless they are forced to do so by those around them. Also, in the case of spiritual direction or guidance, if they seek out this relationship, it is often with someone whom they feel will bless rather than challenge their dysfunctional style.

In general, though, persons seeking support and insight from different types of mentors are much more in tune with their defenses, shortcomings, and personal faults than with their gifts. The problem with this is that in not seeing the blessings they have been given, in terms of attitude and natural talents, they are not able to respond to their true calling in life. Whether it is because of fear of what this might entail or be a form of misplaced modesty, it results in missing the enjoyment of fully experiencing who they are. In addition, those around them miss the gift of their real presence as well. And, since we are with ourselves more than anyone else in life, this is obviously significant.

For Reflection...

> "The Rabbi Zusya said a short time before his death, 'In the world to come, I shall not be asked, "Why were you not Moses?" Instead, I shall be asked, "Why were you no Zusya?"'"
>
> – Martin Buber, *Way of Man*

In Sacred Scripture we see that Abram seemed quite comfortable and generative in his life. Fortunately for him and others he was willing to respond to the call to be Abraham, "the father of his people." Similarly, Sarai, who had probably become accustomed to being barren and was aware of the dangers of pregnancy so late in her life (especially during biblical times) was also willing to become Sarah, a woman filled with new life-giving potential.

But for most of us, the quiet fear is there. We recognize that gifts owned are ones that must be "worked at" and shared, no matter the cost. Once the man crippled from birth who was sitting in front of the temple and living on handouts was cured, his life was changed in more ways than one. The new ability to walk surely must have been exhilarating. However, at some point, as well as discovering and celebrating how he could now walk, run, and leap for joy, he must have finally also realized, "Now, I need to get a job!"

Imago Dei, being made in the image and likeness of God, results in a sense of self that is not impervious to self-doubt, but neither is it totally derailed by it or captured by the limited image that others may have of us. In addition, in our God-given desire for a healthy self-awareness, any psychological damage or spiritual abuse done to us in the past can be faced with clarity and kindness. This allows us to appreciate new healthy experiences that reveal the grater truth about ourselves, others, and God. Tara Westover, in her best-selling book, *Educated*, wrote that, with new positive encounters, "the shame I'd felt about my family leaked out of me almost overnight." The same can be said about the process of *metanoia* when we seek to challenge the inadequate sense of self we might presently be operating under.

As we interact with healthy role models and read, pray over, and challenge scripture we find that our true, more complete image before God becomes more evident. As theologian Karl Barth once said, "When we read scripture and ask, 'What is this book saying?' it should respond in kind and ask, 'Who is it that is asking?'" As we interact with spiritual sages who are more spiritually mature than we are, the psychological storms encountered in uncovering more of the "true self" doesn't remove any psychological blizzard we are facing. Yet, they do provide new "spiritual ski poles" so we can maintain balance and move through the darkness to find deeper inner peace and joy. Moreover, this journey naturally should have an impact on enriching our sense of God as well.

Pat McCloskey in his book *Naming Your God: The Search for Mature Images* wrote,

> Often we drag along behind us images of God—and related images of ourselves and others—that are increasingly heavy. Yet we refuse to leave them behind because we fear that new images might be even heavier in the sense of requiring an even greater conversion on our part. Try as they may, other

> people can only challenge our images, point out self-contradictions, and encourage us to convert, to discover more adequate, more generous, more truthful images about all three. No one else can cut the rope that binds us to images we do not fully trust yet are unwilling to leave behind. The images of God we may be dragging around with great weariness are the same images whether we intend it or not, we are conveying to others.

His points are well-taken, including, maybe *especially* with respect to how *imago Dei* is lived out in us. As is pointed out further in the book *Touching the Holy*:

> If anything then, solid self-esteem based on God's love for us in our ordinariness offers us the real challenge to live nobly and honorably and to help others along the way. Living any other way, with a view of self that is any less than God's view of us, God who wrote our names on the palms of his hands (Is 49:16), is unnecessarily tragic and sad. If we can remember this each day—no matter how we feel or what is facing us—we can then be as spiritually audacious as God has intended us to be all along. And that would be just wonderful, wouldn't it?

And so, the bottom line of spiritual self-awareness is neither self-defacement nor self-worship. It is quite simply to be spiritually intimate in ways that we simultaneously seek the *total* truth about ourselves as we seek knowing more of the truth about God. This is real humility—knowing our gifts and growing edges with a sense of equanimity, and a knowledge that we are not alone. There are people in this world and in our lives, either in person or in books we have treasured, that walk with us. There is also a loving God who does so in ways that contain mystery and new epiphanies about ourselves and the world. And so, given this, what holds us back? What prevents us from accepting ourselves as we are now and seeking to become the most complete going forward? What limits us from letting go of our current self-definition simply as an escape from what we don't like about ourselves and allow it to become an act of passion for God and a desire for a true self-identity that leads to deeper compassion for others? A familiarity with healthy approaches to self-awareness, positive psychology, and narrative therapy can help us in this regard.

Healthy Self-Awareness

Janet Malcom, in "Peeping Through the Keyhole" from Sylvia Platt and Ted Hughes's book *The Silent Woman,* spoke about the biographer at work as a "professional burglar breaking into a house, rifling through certain drawers that he has good reason to think contain jewelry and money, and triumphantly bearing his loot away."

For Reflection...

"Most problems we create because
we don't know ourselves."

– Shunryu Suzuki

The same can be said of the self-awareness search produced by a true spirit of intrigue about ourselves in seeking the true, whole, self. Instead, what often masquerades as such a journey sometimes turns into self-absorption, which true religious wisdom is designed to actually lessen. Part and parcel of such unhealthy self-involvement are the dangers of projection, in which the focus is always on blaming others for our sadness. (As was mentioned this defense is especially "perfected" by persons who are character disordered.) Another danger of looking closely at ourselves is a loss of perspective resulting in our gifts being magnified on the one hand (narcissism) or our faults exaggerated on the other (masochism and neurosis). This can lead to moodiness, discouragement, and anger that comes from an inappropriate and misdirected focus on the self.

With respect to self-absorption, the Dalai Lama is quoted in *The Book of Joy* as saying,

> I think, yes, circumstances, environment, education all matter…especially today; there is not much focus on inner values in education. Then, instead of inner values, we become self-centered—always thinking: *I, I, I.* A self-centered attitude brings a sense of insecurity and fear. Distrust. Too much fear brings frustration. Too much frustration brings anger. So that's the psychology, the system of mind, of emotion, which creates a chain reaction. With a self-centered attitude, you become distanced from others, then distrust, then feel insecure, then fear, then anxiety, then frustration, then anger, then violence.

For many of us, we also have few people in our lives who remember what an original blessing we were in early life to demonstrate and remind us of the gift we have always been and can become even more so going forward. Too often we become enamored of the "lyrics" of life (what a person *does*) rather than the "music" (the true desire for a sense of meaning and fullness in life). As Parker Palmer wrote in *Let Your Life Speak*:

When we lose track of true self, how can we pick up the trail? One way is to seek clues in stories from our younger years, years when we lived closer to our birthright gifts. A few years ago, I found some clues to myself in a time machine of sorts. A friend sent me a tattered copy of my high school newspaper from May 1957 in which I had been interviewed about what I intended to do with my life. With the certainty to be expected of a high school senior, I told the interviewer I would become a naval aviator and then take up a career in advertising.

I was indeed "wearing other people's faces," and I can tell you exactly whose they were. My father worked with a man who had once been a navy pilot. He was Irish, charismatic, romantic, full of the wild blue yonder and a fair share of the blarney, and I wanted to be like him. The father of one of my boyhood friends was in advertising, and though I did not yearn to take on his persona, which was too buttoned-down for my taste, I did yearn for the fast car and other large toys that seemed to be the accessories of his selfhood!

These self-prophecies, now over forty years old, seem wildly misguided for a person who eventually became a Quaker, a would-be pacifist, a writer, and an activist. Taken literally, they illustrate how early in life we can lose track of who we are. But inspected through the lens of paradox, my desire to become an aviator and an advertiser contain clues to the core of true self that would take many years to emerge: clues, by definition, are coded and must be deciphered.

Losing track of our life's desires is easy when we aim for success, comfort, and the admiration and positive response of others. Although these experiences are fine in and of themselves, when they become *primary*, we can, as was previously indicated, lose our way. Yet, the satisfaction that comes from a more complete self-understanding that leads to the intersection of autonomy (our will) and theonomy (God's will) allow us *the inner freedom* that comes from embracing the reality of *imago Dei*, our being made in the image and likeness of God. However, such a pursuit takes true spiritual self-respect. This often requires guidance from someone else who can set the stage for us to develop it in our way, in our time, and in our thoughts and actions in life.

Spiritual Self-Respect—Challenges and Insights from Abraham Joshua Heschel

Once a therapist working with a woman who was sexually abused as a child realized that the three-year therapy with her was ready to be completed. She had learned what she needed to gain new clarity and self-awareness. For it to continue, the therapist knew that it was time to move out of her way, so she could fly on her own.

To accomplish this, he first asked her, "Picture my face as a mirror. What do you see?" She responded by saying, "I see a woman alive with the Spirit. She has resurrected the little girl lost because of the abuse and has now integrated her with the woman she is now...and because of that she is now really something!"

The therapist burst out laughing at this expression of enthusiasm and accomplishment and said, "Yes, you are 'really something' but how did you get to this point? You weren't this way when you first came in to see me." She immediately responded, "Oh, it was easy. The first time I came in to see you, I simply watched how you sat with me and then I began sitting with myself in the same way."

Throughout history, there have been religious figures who have modeled such a sense of respect for the people they were called to guide. In doing this, they have helped them resurrect the person made in the image and likeness of God, rather than the one shaped by the world in its image or disfigured by a theology of sin that psychologically handcuffed them.

An example of such a person is the previously quoted Abraham Joshua Heschel, who was keenly aware of the need and drama of seeking to be made whole so as to live a life of meaning for God and others like all of us are called to be and do. After his death in 1972, one of his disciples said of Heschel, "Perhaps he was a 'lamed Vov,' one of the 36 righteous people of every generation who dwell on the earth anonymously saving it from destruction by their presence." Of the many statements made about him, though, possibly one of the most insightful one was by Jacob Neusner, a distinguished Judaic scholar, who said of him, "To remember him is to learn what we are not but might become."

For Reflection...

> "Everybody is a genius. But if you judge a fish by its ability to climb a tree, it will spend its whole life believing it is stupid."
>
> – Albert Einstein

When a fine work of art is unappreciated, senselessly defaced, or destroyed, there is great sadness and outrage.

However, when an undiscovered, previously forgotten or lost priceless piece is uncovered or recovered, there is a stir of excitement and rippling of joy and gratitude among those who appreciate true beauty. One of Rabbi Heschel's gifts was his keen awareness of these two realities in the case of that often unrecognized, fascinating living works of art we refer to as "the human person." Accordingly, a goal of much of his writing was to bring to light the possibilities of humanity by reminding us that we frequently miss being filled with wonder and awe at the sight of this creation of God. He laments in his book *God in Search of Man* we often forget that a unique fragment of the divine milieu glimmers in our own selves "and sees the things that surround him long before he becomes aware of his own self. Many of us are conscious of the hiddenness of things, but few of us sense the mystery of our own presence."

In *The Insecurity of Freedom*, he recognized that while we may give lip service to the special nature of the human person in creation, there seems to be a lack of full appreciation of the implications of our claims about the unique image that humanity ideally reflects:

> Verbally we seem to be committed to the idea that man is created in the likeness of God. But are we committed to it intellectually? If the divine likeness is our premise, then the question arises: How should a being created in the likeness of God act, think, feel? How should we live in a way which is compatible with our being a likeness of God?

Aristotle once said, "The aim of art is to represent not the outward appearance of the things but their inward significance." So, is it any surprise that when Heschel was asked by an interviewer for NBC-TV shortly before his death, "What message have you for young people?" that he replied very simply and without much difficulty, "Remember that there is meaning beyond absurdity. Know that every deed counts, that every word is power. [And] above all, remember that you must build your life as if it were a work of art."

But children take many of their cues from those older than they are. So, to adults Heschel proposed a similar challenge as to how they should be sensitive to their need to actualize the quiet eminence of their being. He did it by connecting it with the relationship they have with their children. Once again, from his book *The Insecurity of Freedom*, he provides a direct question all of us must face in some way with respect to those who look to us for guidance:

> The Heart of the Ten Commandments is not to be found in the words: *Revere thy father and thy mother.* The problem I as a father face, is why my child should revere me. Unless my child will sense in my personal existence and attitudes that evoke reverence—the ability to delay satisfaction, to overcome prejudice, to sense the holy, to strive for the noble—why should he/she revere me?

The potential grandeur of the human person then for Heschel is a reality. Moreover, it is one which can be seen in our motivations, concrete actions, cognitions (ways of thinking, perceiving, and understanding)...and *choices.* As Heschel recognized,

> All that exists obeys. Man alone occupies a unique status. As a natural being he obeys, as a human being he must frequently choose; confined in his existence, he is unrestrained in his will. His acts do not emanate from him like rays of energy from matter. Placed in the parting of ways, he must time and

again decide which direction to take. The course of his life is, accordingly, unpredictable; no one can write his autobiography in advance.

For some of us, our unique destiny is quite self-evident right from the beginning. Spanish painter, sculptor, printmaker, ceramicist, and theater designer Pablo Picasso was fond of saying, "My mother said to me, 'If you become a soldier, you'll be a general; if you become a monk, you'll end up pope.' Instead, I became a painter and wound up Picasso!" However, even in such cases as this, specific choices are still left to be fashioned by us.

For most of us, the route in life is not clear. We must search the deepest inclinations of our heart to see what our urges and talents are. Then we must not lose our way by pandering to what others would have us be and do. We must not forsake our own momentum in life to respond to God's call to claim the name that is written on his hand in order to follow the call of others' view of success. Still, while this principle is straightforward, it is not easy. The poet e. e. cummings senses this and sums up the tension quite well when he writes, "To be nobody but yourself in a world which is doing its best, night and day, to make you everybody else means to fight the hardest battle which any human being can fight, and never stop fighting."

For Reflection...

"Don't ask yourself what the world needs.
Ask yourself what makes you come alive and
then go do that. Because what the world needs
is people who have come alive."

– Howard Thurman

The fight for Heschel is based on self-respect. It is partially revealed in the previous quote in which he stresses the importance of modeling it for others in our own attitudes and actions. To reiterate, his specific injunctions are "to delay satisfactions, to overcome prejudices, to sense the holy, to strive for the noble."

But how often do we actually do this in life? Does this attitude constantly guide our daily choices, fire the flame of our deep motivations, and provide a theme for a continual sense of commitment to what is of true value rather than merely what is utilitarian or may make us feel good for a while? Once again, in Heschel's own words:

> Man has indeed become primarily a tool-making animal, and the world is now a gigantic toolbox for the satisfaction of his needs.
>
> The Greeks learned in order to comprehend. The Hebrews learned in order to revere. The modern man learns in order to use.... We no longer know how to justify any value except in terms of expediency....

And earlier he states,

> The problem is the spirit of our age: denial of transcendence, the vapidity of values, emptiness in the heart, the decreased sensitivity to the imponderable quality of the spirit, the collapse of communication between the realm of tradition and the inner world of the individual. The central problem is that we do not know how to think, how to pray, how to cry, how to resist the deceptions of too many persuaders.

Heschel also reminds us that as guides for those who would inherit the living rendition and visible covenant with God, the import of *who* we are in their eyes becomes much more compelling than the utterance of a set of unlived dicta—no matter how grand our words may be. Consequently, what Rabbi Heschel descriptively shares in *The Insecurity of Freedom* about "the teacher" of today's youths contains an ideal for *all* adults to keep in mind. It is not simply about us:

> Everything depends on the person who stands in front of the classroom. The teacher is not an automatic fountain from which intellectual beverages may be obtained....He is either a witness or a stranger. To guide a pupil into the promised land, he must have been there himself. When asking himself: Do I stand for what I teach? Do I believe what I say? He must be able to answer in the affirmative.
>
> What we need more than anything else is not *textbooks* but *textpeople*. It is the personality of the teacher which is the text that the pupil reads; the text they will never forget.

Such a personality needs to reflect both self-respect and dedication to what is truly meaningful. If adults do not gratefully recognize the gift from God of the beauty of their own creation, embrace their own gifts, and demonstrate them in their interactions with others, how will young people claim their own noble birth and then live it out? And likewise, if those who offer leadership only seek financial success and don't concern themselves with the search for wisdom, peace, and truth, what lasting message will be heard by, and indelibly impressed upon, those who are positioned to inherit the heart from us?

Psychologically, we can see today that much of the addiction to drugs, power, food, work, success, money, gambling, and physical image is an avoidance of the existential emptiness people feel. Rather than "simply" enjoying the gifts of God, there is a temptation to hold onto them in an effort to create a paradise by our own hands and then follow this by joining with others like us in taking turns to worship ourselves and our accomplishments (narcissism). Yet, Heschel also knew that this delusion, while preventing at times the experience of existential dread, was never a fully convincing one and he expressed this clearly in one of his assessments of the human condition in *Who Is Man?* "Outwardly homo sapiens may pretend to be satisfied and strong; inwardly he is poor, needy, vulnerable, always on the verge of misery, prone to suffer mentally and physically. Scratch his skin and you come upon bereavement, affliction, uncertainty, fear, and pain."

What must we do then? Well, from what has been presented thus far there are at least two important actions that can be taken. The first is to begin—at least at a cognitive level—to find a new sense of self-respect based on the belief that we are *really* made in the image and likeness of God so we can reflect on what particular gifts we have been given that support this reality. This effort in true self-understanding of our unique reflection of creation can then help us move away from the often-religious, guilt-ridden self-condemnation that results from comparing ourselves (often unconsciously in an unfavorable way) with others. This makes way for a *new* search for what is already positively alive in our personalities and talents (both major and minor) that must be further enhanced as a way to more fully become ourselves. To accomplish this, we must have deep gratitude for what is especially beautiful in us, take steps to foster the development of our strengths, and then attempt to uncover those instances when we "psychologically trip over" them because of unnecessary anxiety or loss of confidence.

For example, some of us are passionate, energetic, and achievement oriented. And this is good as much can be done that is positive with such energy and commitment. However, when we doubt ourselves, and fail to see the presence of God in ourselves, rather than freely and openly expressing these gifts from God, we run the risk of trying to be "a god" on our own. Thus, our enthusiasm may change into exhibitionism, and our achievement-oriented behavior may sink into a destructive form of competitiveness. This, in turn, may feed the long-term negative feelings we have about ourselves even though the temporary secondary gain may offer us a partial denial/avoidance of our fears.

One psychological way to follow Heschel's urgings and counter this destructive movement is through the use of imagery. In the morning, and during breaks in the day, a few moments of vivid reflection on ourselves as persons made in the image and likeness of God in general, and a specific recollection of the concrete ways this is so, will serve to better center us on our human nobility based on God's love and generosity to us. This will increase the chance that we will recognize where and how we have gone astray. As Thomas Merton once noted, you don't have to worry about a public or even an ideal image when you are a friend of God. We will then cease being lost in an "emotional desert" that comes from the nostalgic, misplaced longing for the so-called security of some particular talent we alone feel we are responsible for or the wish to be extraordinary and worthy of special attention by others because of this. This can open us then to return to an awe of self-appreciation and self-respect tempered by the humility arising from a deep belief we are blessed because of God's faithfulness to, and encouragement of, us—*not* based on our work alone.

Along with setting time aside to image the divine in ourselves, so that we can model healthy self-respect for others through our growing sense of spiritual maturity, we can also image the divine in the world in concrete, possibly new ways. In pursuit of this, we seek to connect the immediate with the ultimate so as to rejoice, respect, and be glad.

For Reflection...

"What difference does it make if the bread and wine turn into the Body and Blood of Christ, if we don't?"

– Godfrey Diekmann, OSB

Appreciating the blessedness of nobility does not mean that we should be blinded to evil in ourselves or miss the tendency to project it only on to others. It also is not the naïve belief that embracing nobility conceptually is tantamount to actually achieving it once and for all. There must be a willingness to continually evaluate our actions in light of the theme of self-respect with the question: How am I uncovering and sharing the divine in my attitudes, choices, and actions with respect to how I behave toward others?

Whereas this is not a question primarily designed to instill guilt (although guilt may initially be needed at times to break through the crust of our denial), it is certainly one created to help us *remember*. Remember what? Remember that the covenant we have with God as people truly made in the divine image and likeness is *not to be taken lightly*. This is the case both individually and systemically. Swiss psychiatrist Carl Jung once quipped, "The brighter the light...the deeper the darkness." On a broader level, Germany before WWII was filled with persons of great wisdom and accomplishment. Yet, the holocaust happened. The United States in the twenty-first century contained people of great generosity and talent but wound up becoming divided and marked by the shouts of people of greed and hostility in places of power—including the church. As sociologist Kyriaco Markides notes in his book *Gifts of the Desert*:

Quiet Dangers

> Institutionalization in a religious movement is an unavoidable and necessary development if a religion is to survive over decades and centuries. During this process, however, people who may not be motivated by purely spiritual considerations can join and climb up the church hierarchy. Sociologists have a special term for this development: the "dilemma of mixed emotions."

And so, attention to uncovering our own signature strengths—including the lesser ones—and examining our story to ensure it is not dictated by someone or something other than God, is essential for us and our community. Moreover, in support of this process, we need more than good intentions and strong motivation. We need knowledge that will help both persons and communities to image, discover more deeply, and live compassionately by appreciating psychologically what *imago Dei* truly can mean for individuals and the world in which they live. To help in this regard, we now have both positive psychology and narrative therapy as partial supports for how we may proceed to embrace more fully a divine call rather than simply settling for a worldly call that is insufficient and possibly even dangerous to the way we live and to those we meet along the way.

2. The Exhilarating Psychological Search for *Imago Dei*

CBT, Positive Psychology, and Narrative Therapy

There is a true spiritual call for us to unearth and share the unique sense of ourselves that we believe reflects being made in the image and likeness of God (*imago Dei*). In the words of contemplative, Thomas Merton, "To say that I am made in the image of God is to say that Love is the reason for my existence, for God is love. Love is my true identity; selflessness is my true self. Love is my true character. Love is my name." In pursuit of this, there are now psychological approaches designed to help us in this journey. Their goal is to unlock the psychological and social handcuffs that society and those close to us may have put on us that have affected our outlook about ourselves. We often leave these perspectives unexamined and unchallenged and continue to believe.

Obviously, it is important for us to have an accurate self-image, so we don't dismiss the positive feedback we receive or miss the signature strengths we have. If we do see ourselves in a balanced way, we can be freer and more integrated. Moreover, recognizing and accepting our talents, we are in a stronger position to be compassionate to many different types of people, no matter how they react to us. This will save psychic energy instead of wasting it on trying to develop several personalities or on feeling we must don different defensive masks depending upon whom we are with. Seeing our gifts more clearly will also help us to develop more fully as persons because we will be able to tend to them and share them more effectively with others in the brief time we are on earth.

In addition, it will help us to better monitor the meaning or messages we give ourselves all day. This is referred to in psychology as "self-talk" or what I prefer to call quiet "self-whispers," since they often go unrecognized and therefore unexamined or unchallenged—especially when they should be carefully examined because, quite simply, they are wrong! With a real sense of self, we can approach situations with a greater sense of certainty and humility. Consequently, rather than feeling we need to always seek approval or reinforcement (though some is natural and good), we can act out of our true identity. If positive results occur, fine; if negative ones occur, well, fine too, because—with a healthy perspective—they will all teach us something if examined carefully, *with the right spirit*. As thirteenth-century poet Rumi aptly notes, "If light is in your heart, you will find your way home."

In the spirit of valuing *imago Dei*, when we feel ourselves becoming anxious, depressed, or stressed, we can ask questions that will get us back in touch with our true calling. This will help us to see that our fears and "dis-ease" are arising out of playing a role, fearing rejection, or being revealed as a charlatan of some type. To help us counter this, some questions we need to ask ourselves when having negative feelings include:

- Why am I making myself so anxious or angry in this situation?
- What is it about this situation that is making me so uncomfortable?
- What do I fear losing in this situation?

- What am I demanding of the people around me, and why is it so upsetting that I am not getting it?
- What is the worst thing that could happen if I said or did ________?
- Why am I so worried about the possibility of people seeing me as imperfect, unhelpful, a failure, not unique, self-seeking, self-protecting, greedy, addicted, or ignorant? At some level isn't this at least somewhat true?
- What is the reason I am giving people the power to upset me?
- What is the most helpful thing I can do in this instance to learn about myself and the people and situation at hand?
- If I am alone, what is it that I am concentrating on in myself that is transforming solitude into loneliness and self-deprecation?
- Why am I taking a possibly annoying event and making it into something worse?

All of the above basic questions, which we often don't stop to ask ourselves, can help free us from wasteful ways of thinking that lead to an unhealthy perspective. We can be more content with ourselves as we travel our psychological and spiritual journeys in life. These questions are designed to break the logjam of unrealistic expectations, unnecessary fears, crippling angers, destructive anxieties, and undue distress. Then it becomes possible to live with greater clarity, contentment, and compassion. The questions also produce a good deal of information on how we are falling into patterns of pleasing, grasping, and controlling rather than living out of our central identity ("name") and simply flowing with our lives.

For Reflection...

"Meaning is something you build into your life. You build it out of your own past, out of your affections and loyalties, out of the experience of humankind as it is passed on to you.... You are the only one who can put them together into that unique pattern that will be your life."

– John Gardner, Civic Leader
Address to the Stanford Alumni Association

The freedom to live with a healthier perspective has a cost though. The price is *honesty* and *humility*. Without these, we are not clear about what is before us, we fail to be content, and we often lack the purity of motivations to help us be compassionate without wanting anything in return. Yes, there is a cost, but the serenity that results is truly worth the effort. If we are aware that we have been given myriad talents (some not yet explored), as an act of gratitude for possessing them we can seek to enhance and share them as best as we can. The process allows us to never, ever forget they are in fact originally genetic *gifts*, and so we can be excited and content to be who we are without a drop of conceit—which will also be a gift to others who encounter us. In support of this, three major areas of clinical psychology that I have discussed in my book *Perspective: The Calm within the Storm* can be of assistance: cognitive-behavioral theory, positive psychology, and narrative therapy.

Cognitive-Behavioral Theory (CBT)

Cognitive behavioral therapy is designed to provide great insights into why people feel the way they do and how both affect (mood) and behaviors are determined to a great extent by their cognitions (ways of thinking, perceiving, and understanding) and schemata (beliefs). Given this, as part of our daily journeys, CBT advises people that in seeking a healthier perspective, daily effort also needs to be made in today's anxious world to carefully examine our own cognitions to see what distortions might be present that may be causing us difficulties.

Cognitive behavioral therapy recognizes that psychological problems are often negatively impacted by dysfunctional thinking. Originally developed by Aaron Beck in the 1960s, this short-term, structured psychotherapy was first used with clients suffering from depression but has since been expanded to include areas such as other mood disorders, trauma, substance abuse, and the improvement of everyday living. The major assumption of CBT is that life experiences create core beliefs and schemas (underlying beliefs that provide a way of responding based on relationship to self, others, and the world). These, in turn, drive intermediate tenets, which are personal rules, attitudes, and assumptions. And so, when an incident occurs, automatic thoughts are generated that impact behavior and mood.

Cognitive behavioral theory and therapy can be helpful because there is a bias for action and an emphasis on working with the present as a way to alleviate the symptoms of psychic distress as quickly as possible. As a result, we are invited by this theory to identify (by ourselves or with a wise friend or coach) a dysfunctional cognition based on a core belief and to work on decreasing negative affect while increasing coping skills related to the negative, unexamined, automatic thoughts we may have: in essence, to seek a healthier perspective.

Distorted thoughts can come in a variety of different forms. Examples include *catastrophizing* (I am going to lose everything), *magnifying* (this is the worst thing that could ever happen to me), *overgeneralizing* (everyone thinks this way about me), *jumping to conclusions*, *selective negative focus*, *emotional reasoning*, "*shoulds*," *polarized* or *all or nothing thinking* (if we don't do it my way, it is wrong) and *personalizing* (he doesn't like me because I didn't go out to lunch with him). While many people may fall into using this type of unexamined, negative thinking from time to time, it becomes especially problematic when it becomes the default way of thinking, which unfortunately may happen when we are at a low point during life. Yet, whether it is extreme or not, for all of us, dysfunctional thinking is certainly detrimental to possessing a healthy perspective in life.

Negative thinking is more common than we might think. We often hear praise in a whisper and negative feedback as thunder; it is easier to give more weight to a negative interpretation than to anything positive. Often, we can hear a compliment or affirmation only to have it dissolve when negative stones are thrown and hit their mark. Thus, it is important that we be educated to pick up and recognize negative thinking in order to link it to depressive or anxious feelings that may result. Then, the negative self-talk can be replaced with a more realistic thought or belief. (In addition, as we shall soon see, the use of accurate positive language is also central to helping us make changes.)

Generally, it is easy to find something negative about ourselves and even easier to make negative comparisons with others. On the other hand, maintaining a healthy perspective in light of these challenges—even though it can be an extremely worthwhile endeavor—is where the real work begins. Once again, as Rainer Maria Rilke, in one of his *Letters to a Young Poet*, offers:

> Only someone who is ready for everything, who excludes nothing, not even the most enigmatical, will live the relation to another as something alive and will himself draw exhaustively from his own existence. For if we think of this existence of the individual as a

> larger or smaller room it appears evident that most people learn to know only one corner of their room, a place by the window, a strip of floor on which they will walk up and down. Thus they have a certain security. And yet that dangerous insecurity is so much more human which drives the prisoner in Poe's stories to feel out the shapes of their horrible dungeons and not be strangers to the unspeakable terror of their abode. We, however, are not prisoners. No traps or snares are set about us, and there is nothing which should intimidate or worry us.... We have no reason to mistrust our world, for it is not against us. Has it terrors, they are our terrors; has it abysses, those abysses belong to us; are dangers at hand, we must try to love them.

To accomplish this form of self-awareness, so change becomes more readily possible, a number of steps can be taken either by ourselves or with a therapist, coach, mentor, or counselor. They include exploring the cognitive appraisal of an event; revisiting the emotional arousal it caused; and examining the resulting behavior that one undertook. As part of this recollecting process, it is important that both the objective (what actually happened) and the subjective (what beliefs and judgments one has made about the event) be examined. With this process the person can then be encouraged to uncover the style of their thinking process as well as examine the accuracy of the conclusions being made.

Positive Psychology

With a sense of the value of CBT as a backdrop, another even more recent advance in the behavioral sciences that can be helpful—especially with respect to gaining a more balanced, fuller view of self, and in the process gain a healthier perspective—is *positive psychology*. Its goal is to encourage the field of clinical psychology not to see itself as merely being a "repair shop" for emotional difficulties (as important as this role is) but also to help people uncover their signature strengths. By drawing attention to their gifts, talents, and virtues, people can build upon what is good instead of solely focus on correcting what is problematic. This enhances resiliency, which is an area that is not of little concern to those wishing to have a healthier perspective and live a full, refreshing, and compassionate life.

The discipline of positive psychology is about living well. It is prevention focused and works to expand existing competencies. It looks at people's past experiences and how they have adapted to become who they are today. It also examines their sense of personal contentment, and how their attitudes and optimism influence their future. By taking this perspective, people are encouraged to question themselves in a whole new more holistic way. (As was previously noted, people—and those who guide them—are sometimes stuck looking solely at their shortcomings while neglecting the power of their innate talents and gifts. Positive psychology seeks to correct this imbalance.)

According to Martin Seligman, initiator of the contemporary positive psychology movement and author of *Authentic Happiness: Using Positive Psychology to Realize Your Potential for Lasting Fulfillment*:

> The field of positive psychology at the subjective level is about positive subjective experience: well-being and satisfaction (past); flow, joy, the sensual pleasures, and happiness (present); and constructive cognitions about the future—optimism, hope, and faith. At the individual level it is about positive personal

> traits—the capacity for love and vocation, courage, interpersonal skill, aesthetic sensibility, perseverance, forgiveness, originality, future-mindedness, high talent, and wisdom....Psychology is not just the study of disease, weakness, and damage; it also is the study of strength and virtue. Treatment is not just fixing what is wrong; it is also building what is right....The major strides in prevention have largely come from a perspective focused on systematically building competency, not correcting weakness....This, then, is the general stance of positive psychology toward prevention. It claims that there is a set of buffers against psychopathology: the positive human traits.

Positive psychology is not a psychological concealer that hides the real blemishes of life, nor is it an emotional or spiritual cortisone that temporarily eliminates unpleasant life experiences. Instead, it is a more dynamic way for people to view their state of being and be freed from the bindings of a solely negative focus. Although positive psychology is centered upon the individual, it also integrates the strengths of supporting institutions such as families, schools, and religious institutions.

Positive and negative emotions are designed to have specific purposes in our lives. Too much of one without the other to balance it could be problematic. Christopher Peterson, the author of *A Primer on Positive Psychology*, noted that

> negative emotions alert us to danger. When we experience a negative emotion, our response options narrow, and we act with haste to avoid whatever danger is signaled. In contrast, positive emotions signal safety, and our inherent response to them is not to narrow our options but to broaden and build upon them. The evolutionary payoff of positive emotions

> is therefore not in the here and now, but in the future. Perhaps it is advantageous to experience positive emotions because they lead us to engage in activities that add to our behavioral and cognitive repertoires.

Research has also shown that a positive outlook can contribute to longer, healthier lives, richer marriages, more productive work environments, and closer friendships. In addition, this optimism improves resilience, strengthens coping skills, and moves people from survival to enrichment—a movement that is clearly essential if we are to have, and live out of, a healthy perspective.

One way to measure the richness of life is to consider the impact of "flow." Identified by Mihaly Csikszentmihalyi (in his book of the same name), this psychological state of being is the overlap of refined skill, single-mindedness, and joy. For individuals who experience flow, time seems to stand still, there is no self-consciousness, and the activity brings a sense of completeness. By embarking on a discovery process that highlights our most rewarding activities and encourages a steady diet of them, we are better able to help ourselves (and others who seek our support) tap into the positive energy in and around us.

Employing positive psychology as a tool in seeking a healthier perspective on a reflective grid then should center on experiences, events, behaviors, cognitions, gifts, talents, and conditions to be recalled, celebrated, and reinforced—not just on our problems, defenses, and growing edges, as important as awareness of them might be.

Deriving honest meaning from our experiences and testing our perceptions can offer a freedom that may be unknown or elusive up to that point because of the negative beliefs held. And so, it is with having both cognitive behavioral therapy and positive psychology as a backdrop (see resources on these areas listed at the end of the book) that we wish now to briefly discuss the concepts of *reframing and change and signature strengths* to see how they can be applied to gaining, maintaining, or regaining a healthy perspective.

Reframing for Change

Cognitive reframing is an intervention that helps a person create new meaning from distressing situations where irrational, distorted, or imbalanced thinking has affected their behavior or mood, or both. With the collaboration of a psychological guide or—as in the case of the goal of this book—on one's own, maladaptive thoughts or narrow ways of viewing events are identified, and new ideas are generated to allow both perception (and ultimately both feeling and behavior) and our perspective to be modified even though the precipitating event actually remains the same.

Most dysfunctional thinking styles have taken a lifetime to develop, and persons need adequate space to consider a reconceptualization of their thinking and beliefs. This cycle of cognitive appraisal, emotional arousal, and behavior is also continuous. Once again, the goal of reframing for change is not designed to deny realities but *to look into them with a sense of openness and hope—a different perspective.* It is to help raise recognition where we are in the cycle of change and bring it into clearer focus. With that awareness, we can begin connecting our maladaptive thoughts and incomplete or inaccurate personal assumptions. And by practicing reframing in and outside of the reflective periods of "alone-time" in our day, we can derive new insights and enhance personal well-being.

The fundamental components of reframing our perspective in practice are:

- To hear what we are and are not saying to ourselves (self-talk);
- To acknowledge what we are feeling;
- To help ourselves gain insight into the *full* experience.

Often, we debate whether the glass is half-full or half-empty. In reframing, our interest is in the entire glass, both the represented signature strengths *and* our defenses or growing edges. The goal is not to hide or play down the defenses or situational challenges but to recognize them for what they are while *simultaneously* applauding the gifts in all parts of ourselves or members of our family or those who turn to us at work for guidance.

For Reflection...

"From the beginning, our lives lay down clues to selfhood and vocation, though the clues may be hard to decode. But trying to interpret them is profoundly worthwhile—especially when we are in our twenties or thirties or forties, feeling profoundly lost, having wandered, or been dragged, far away from our birthright gifts."

– Parker Palmer, *Let Your Life Speak*

Just as mattes and frames can bring different details to the foreground in a painting, in utilizing CBT and positive psychology, the practice of seeking a perspective that is more accurate and life giving allows us to recast certain details of our story or shed light on our faulty beliefs. And just as viewing a painting from a variety of angles brings perspective, we become an observer of the "paintings" (stories in our own life) in order to help ourselves become more fully self-aware. This is done in order to secure or regain personal power, as well as to adopt new contexts for perceiving events in particular and our life as a whole.

The process of reframing benefits from both being open and having a good sense of humor. In addition, a relationship with persons who are explicitly familiar with CBT and positive psychology or are individuals who are very balanced and healthy in their own view of life, is essential. Although there are many psychological theories and techniques that can be used to help people lead a more fruitful, satisfying life, studies have shown that it is the *relationship* between the helper and the person being guided that plays the most significant role in healing. Thus, rapport and a sense of trust are critical. And so, having a companion (either in person or via their writings) who is able to help us become aware of *both* our gifts and our growing edges is a special gift to us when we are seeking a healthier perspective on ourselves and our lives.

This is so because when we are psychologically stuck it can sometimes be difficult to decipher where we are in terms of gifts and growing edges. Therefore, an open mind is also essential. From a psychological and spiritual point of view, the difficulty we may be experiencing is often not really the "complete problem," so constant reconceptualizing through reflection or within a coaching or mentoring relationship needs to take place. By embracing an open "what if" mentality, some of the potential challenges experienced can be illuminated when new possibilities are explored. In addition, sometimes minor events in our life can be taken far too seriously. By employing humor appropriately, a logjam of emotions can be released so self-examination doesn't become something too burdensome or off-putting.

CBT and positive psychology are evidence-based theories that have been tested. With practice on self and others, they can add a new dimension to the search for a healthier perspective on our part or in support of others on their life journey. These theories also offer a new path of exploration which may be uncharted, so gentle persistence may be necessary because there will be steps forward and back during the entire process of seeking greater openness and flexibility to change. And finally, we must not forget that no matter how efficacious our approach, it is, in the end, about *experiencing* the gifts of life wherever and whenever they appear. We are imperfect and our best intentions may fall short. Life tends to bridge those gaps and enriches the shared journey by encouraging us all to be open to "make all things new," including, maybe *especially*, ourselves as life changes and develops.

A story once told about author Franz Kafka expresses this beautifully. Kafka, who never married or had children encountered a little girl in a Berlin park. She was crying and he asked her why she was so sad. It turned out that she had lost her doll and it led to Kafka being willing to look for it with her. They failed to find it that day and on the next day when they tried again. However, Kafka was prepared for this situation and gave her a letter he prepared that was purportedly written by the doll. It said that she shouldn't cry because she took a trip to see the world and that she would write to her about the adventures.

Kafka then wrote a series of enchanting letters from the doll that the little girl loved. Finally, he then bought a doll for the little girl and gave it to her to which she responded that the doll didn't look like hers after all. To which Kafka responded by giving her a letter, which said simply, "My travels have changed me."

Our travels in life have also changed us. Therefore, it is important that we discover who we are now after all the experiences and encounters we have had. One of the best ways to do this is to uncover *all* our signature strengths—not simply ones that others have told us about or value in a way that has had us emphasize them with more vigor. In this way, we will also increase our chances of seeing clearly—not only ourselves as we were created to be and develop, but also, others, life...*and God.*

Signature Strengths

Although there are many aspects of positive psychology that can help provide such a basis for insight into this focus, one of the main ones related to gaining and maintaining a healthier perspective—which will be provided here as an example—is helping ourselves and those who turn to us in our interpersonal circle, to better unearth and cultivate our and their strengths.

Clifton and Hodges helped in this regard by providing the following definition of a strength as "the ability to provide consistent, near-perfect performance in a given activity. The key to building a strength is to first identify your dominant themes of talent, then to discover your specific talents within those themes, and lastly to refine them with knowledge and skills."

Some strengths and talents may be readily apparent such as the student who can organize and lead a group of individuals to accomplish a task, whether it is a science lab or a campus-wide rally. Another may be able to electrify an audience, because of his ability to speak clearly and passionately about his area of interest or expertise. Yet, for others, personality clues may have to be sorted to determine predominant strengths. Buckingham and Clifton, for example, in their work cite spontaneous reactions, yearnings, rapid learning, and satisfaction as the individual's possible ways of identifying talent. In other words, what are the individual's gut reactions, what are they drawn to doing, how quickly can they pick up a new skill, and what makes them happy?

A resource designed by Peterson and Seligman, called the *Character Strengths and Virtues Classification System*, is worth consulting as well, since it offers a means of assessment in positive psychology. Specifically naming and deliberately cultivating what is inherently good in those who are in formation contributes to their resilience, meaning, and happiness. Briefly, the system isolates seven key characteristics of a strength that are: consistently evident and stable over time; valued by society; nurtured by caregivers; promoted through structured institutions such as schools; identified as role models, as well as prodigies; and recognized and highly considered by most major cultures.

In Peterson and Seligman's guide, six virtues are identified and divided into twenty-four subcategories representing character strengths:

- *Wisdom and Knowledge* combined represent the mental fitness to solicit and utilize information. Suggested strengths include curiosity, interest; love of learning; judgment, critical thinking, open-mindedness; practical intelligence, creativity, originality, ingenuity, and perspective.
- *Courage* is the emotional tenacity that drives achievement regardless of the obstacles. Strengths highlighted are in the areas of valor, industry, perseverance, integrity, honesty, authenticity, zest, and enthusiasm.
- *Love* is self-sacrifice for another. Strengths involve intimacy, reciprocal attachment; kindness, generosity, nurturance; social intelligence, personal intelligence, and emotional intelligence.
- *Justice* references the desire to complete civic duties that contribute to the larger whole. This includes citizenship, duty, loyalty, teamwork; equity, fairness, and leadership.

- *Temperance* refrains from excess and includes strengths such as forgiveness, mercy; modesty, humility; prudence, caution; self-control and self-regulation.
- *Transcendence* ties to that which is greater than the self and gives humankind purpose. Strengths include awe, wonder, appreciation of beauty and excellence, gratitude, hope, optimism, future-mindedness, playfulness, humor, spirituality, sense of purpose, faith, and religiousness.

This list represents a framework for further discussion. In line with this, a sampling of the interventions to strengthen positive traits described by Peterson and Seligman are noted as follows:

- Brainstorming ideas for an express purpose promotes creativity.
- Taking risks, adapting, and questioning are ways of building courage.
- Incorporating fun encourages perseverance.
- Participating in community service promotes social responsibility.
- Practicing forgiveness of self and others is how not to be trapped in the past.
- Offering accurate feedback encourages humility and modesty, if it is stated in a manner that allows the individual to grow.
- Laughing brings about playfulness.
- Thanking others grows gratitude.

Many of these activities can be expanded to include a larger community whether it is our extended family, the workplace, or an institution (church, school, and the like) in which we are involved.

The questions in Peterson and Seligman's guide are designed to inspire self-exploration and whet the appetite to delve further into the subject. The mere practice of identifying strengths and offering examples of how they have been used can be extremely gratifying especially during tough times. It is also good to be reminded of all the gifts that we have because some that can still be of great value to us may have fallen out of practice.

The ability for people to be proficient at something—or perhaps even be an expert—can contribute to happiness and well-being. Thus, uncovering our strengths, as well as finding ways in which we can employ our talents in daily life, is essential for instilling confidence and supporting mastery. Dieter Frey developed his own principles of leadership and motivation that highlighted central themes that positively influenced employee satisfaction and performance in the workplace. These principles are an outgrowth of human strengths and offer a framework for another way of intervening not only in our own life but with others as well.

Likewise, the questions that follow can offer a valuable source of direct application and ongoing introspection. The principles are as follows:

- *Providing meaning and vision*: People who perceive their work as having a greater purpose and tied to a larger strategy are more motivated and enthusiastic about what they do. (How do we see our role as helpers to others? How do our particular strengths benefit our family, friends, school, religious organization, or workplace? How clearly are we able to link our actions to the broader strategy of organizations of which we are a part?)

- *Transparency*: Being informed helps people to have a sense of control and provides a framework for change. (Are the discussions with others in the family, community, or workplace open and honest? Can constructive criticism be shared and valued? Is this echoed in our organization?)
- *Participation and autonomy*: People who actively contribute to the decision-making process are more likely to assume responsibility. (What are the expectations of any mentoring-type relationship of which we are a part? Are we invested and willing to work diligently together with those who guide us or with those whom we are called to guide?)
- *Sense of fit*: If people understand their strengths and use them to do the work they love, they will be more motivated to keep doing it. (Do we have the skills necessary and the interest? What are our motivations? Are they a good fit for the type of work we do and the family life we have?)
- *Goal setting and goal negotiation*: People who establish reasonable goals and develop a plan to meet them tend to be more motivated. (Are there specific goals established for our personal development? Is there enough flexibility to reevaluate the goals as necessary and enough resources to accomplish what we have laid out?)
- *Constructive feedback and appreciation*: People want to do well and be recognized. Likewise, positive correction builds up people and their skills. (Is there room for our ongoing appraisal individually? Is this support echoed in our place of work?)

- *Professional and social integration*: People want to be part of a community and acknowledged for their contributions. (How is this need fulfilled in our life at this point? How do we model having a healthy perspective in our life?)
- *Personal growth*: People want to expand their skills and knowledge. (How are we encouraging personal growth in ourselves?)
- *Situational leadership*: Leadership style is adaptable to the event and should be clear and directive. (How are we seeking to enhance our own strengths as leaders in our family? With various community organizations? At work?)
- *Fair and equitable material reward*: This suggests that rewards should be clearly articulated and commensurate with the investment. (What are the tangible and intangible rewards of having a more positively balanced view of ourselves and the world?)

I have suggested exploratory questions to guide personal reflection about growth, mastery, and contentment. This rich body of information can be leveraged throughout our own personal development process and beyond. Several applications follow, including:

- Doing a holistic self-assessment that includes our gifts as well as our growing edges;
- Making a choice with an appreciation that we just don't think our way into a new kind of thinking but must also act our way into a new kind of living (as the Twelve Steps of AA would suggest);
- Practicing new behavior that will encourage growth and openness;

- Paying it forward by behaving toward others as we now are behaving toward ourselves;
- Partnering with others who are models of persons who seem to maintain or regain a healthy perspective when it becomes temporarily lost; and
- Viewing each day as the last since such an appreciation of our own impermanence encourages us not to get caught in petty struggles.

Although there are benefits to doing these activities individually, they can also be designed to be done collectively so new discoveries can be made and ongoing refinement occurs.

Conducting an honest self-assessment is also a foundational step to using positive psychology in an effort to gain a healthier perspective on self and the world. A fair appraisal of strengths, growing edges, and attitude is necessary to make minute and incremental improvements. Given this, how do I respond to such questions as:

- Do we characterize life as full of opportunity or a problem to endure?
- If a positive mindset is the wiring in place, then how do we determine if it is consistent across all domains or if there are situations or individuals that are draining?
- If we become exhausted, how can our interactions be limited or changed going forward to create better outcomes?
- If a negative mindset is more the norm for us at a given point, do we remember that cognitive "rewiring" takes time, care, and patience but is well worth the effort?

Choice is another key driver in using positive psychology and the development of a healthier perspective. In other words, we need to intentionally choose to employ strengths in life and use the lens of positivity to view all that happens. Often people are trapped in a thought process that says, "I have to do it this way," or "If I can just survive this, I can get to the next better thing." This thought process influences our behavior consciously and unconsciously. We may procrastinate, worry about something that is out of our control, or be wrought with anxiety that far outweighs the actual situation. In essence, we are robbing ourselves of joy when we do not recognize that we can govern our behavior.

Using Signature Strengths

Take a moment to consider all of the things that are "obligations" on the calendar. How can they become opportunities to learn something new, nourish, and grow another individual? Also, consider what is done well and *liked*. Many people can be trained to do things so well that they can be perceived as strengths. However, they may not enjoy spending hours in those activities. This is often true in the workplace where people must adapt to retain their employment. Thus, determine how more time can be spent doing activities that utilize signature strengths. For example, being a mentor to colleagues energizes some, while for others ensuring they are at their children's sport or club event gives them meaning.

Practicing is still another key concept. Cultivating strengths by employing them often and using them in unique ways is critical. In addition, it is helpful to consider how a positive attitude impacts the way a strength is used or how a negative attitude may minimize what is inherently good. It is easy for us to start complaining when everyone else in the room is doing so and to be swept away by hopelessness in difficult, tragic, or chronic situations. Yet, those individuals who can draw something of value from any situation tend to do better and remain healthier than those who cannot. And so, it is not Pollyannaish (as some may claim) to practice looking for the good in self, others, and events. A simple example: weather often brings about a lot of comments, usually negative—but it doesn't have to be this way.

Whenever possible, including others by *paying it forward* is a wonderfully beneficial way to put positive psychology to use in our own lives as well as in others. Strengths used to benefit a community tend to grow because they are called upon more frequently and praised. Likewise, individuals who can highlight the strengths of others are in a position to potentially give gifts of immeasurable worth. Family, friends, colleagues, and even those who we meet in passing in our lives may surprisingly share great hurts. At the same time, they may also be receiving very few nurturing supports from those in their interpersonal network. Whenever we can help them see their courage for sharing with us, their tenacity for continuing, their willingness to be open, and their strength in working through their challenges, it may be instrumental in beginning the healing process for them—and a powerful way to develop the signature strengths in ourselves!

Most of us have a unique opportunity to pour into others abundantly but because of our perspective on the "*helping* process" we may miss out on those small but possibly significant moments. Small daily steps can matter in surprising ways if we don't simply think about good acts but actually do them. By way of example, complimenting at least one person a day about something that makes them special can have an unexpected positive impact.

One way of doing this is looking at the details. Does a friend wear a hat celebrating his service to our country or an organization pin on her lapel? Both suggest a willingness to sacrifice and serve others, which are incredible gifts. Another way is catching a person in the act of doing something positive or beneficial. For example, a gentle and generous colleague of mine was out to dinner with her family and saw a young father with three boys ranging from around ages five to ten. It was a busy evening, and they waited a long time for their food. As she and her family left, she complimented the father and his sons on how impressed she was with their kind and caring behavior to each other. Dad sat up a bit straighter and thanked her. Each of the boys beamed. That was a fleeting interaction, but for those few moments she and they enjoyed what was strong and good in their family—and in her, since she manifested one of her own signature strengths: demonstrated compassion for others.

Similarly, there are many people around who would be pleased to share what they know and *partner with us* as well. The easiest way to improve upon a particular strength is by joining another who desires the same. If positivity is a struggle, we also need to spend time with people who have a healthier perspective than we do. Consider how they act, speak, and carry themselves. Observe how they make others feel when they are with them. Then we need to take the further effort to adapt and imitate what they do. We may find this to be awkward at first, but it will become more natural over time.

Finally, *view each day as the last.* Our lives are finite, yet we often act as if they are eternal. We allow anger to fester, deny forgiveness, and foster dysfunction. We toss away precious moments surfing the net or watching television instead of investing in relationships. Would that be true if we knew that this was our last day on earth? Chances are a few things would change, and we would focus on making good memories and getting closure. And so, we need to make a commitment to stop and be mindful throughout the day; choose to operate from a source of strength; and, finally, select words and act in ways that build others up, not pull them down.

For Reflection...

"You don't have to be worthy;
you only have to be willing."

– St. Padre Pio

By integrating aspects of positive psychology, including contentment, growth, and mastery, into our own selves, as well as in significant relationships, gifts of untold value may be unwrapped through gaining a balanced (*both* gifts and growing edges) picture of those who come to us for guidance as well as ourselves. Seeking to have a more balanced, fuller view of self can also be an opportunity to identify and sharpen strengths and sets the stage further to expand the story we have of ourselves (our "narrative")—in other words, given the particular focus of this book, gain a healthier perspective on self and, in turn, those we encounter. A few lessons from the narrative therapy literature can help in this regard.

Narrative Therapy

At each phase of our lives—not just once and for all—we need to ensure that a healthier perspective on life includes the way we view *ourselves* rather than simply mimicking what others say about us. Parker Palmer, in his book *Let Your Life Speak*, attests to this as he reflects on even the favorable elements of his own life when he notes, "The life I am living is not the same as the life that wants to live in me....I had started to understand that it is indeed possible to live a life other than one's own....I had simply found a 'noble' way to live that was not my own, a life spent imitating heroes instead of listening to my heart."

On a more dramatic note, actress Liv Ullman once shared the following related, deeply felt sentiment regarding her own narrative:

> I am learning that if I just go on accepting the framework for life that others have given me, if I fail to make my own choices, the reasons for my life will be missing. I will be unable to recognize that which I have the power to change. I refuse to spend my life regretting the things I failed to do.

Given this potential reality and in line with positive psychology, another very creative approach to achieving a healthier, richer sense of self and ability in the process of helping others gain a more complete sense of self is *narrative therapy*.

Narrative therapy as a process is associated with the groundbreaking work of Michael White and David Epston. They were interested in how people's life stories attributed to them, but not by them, were problematic. In one of their key maxims, "the person is not the problem, the problem is the problem." And the problem is a function of a labeling that overshadows alternative stories of possibility that the person has within themselves but may not be in touch with at the time.

Narrative therapy encourages the very skills that all of us need to have in opening up our perspective as to who we are, who we can be, and how we might live each day as well as with respect to vocation and long-term goals. These include:

- Listening to our hopes, dreams, and ideas so they are not eclipsed or crushed by the attitudes of culture, family, work, or our own previously limited self-definition.
- Reflecting on those "little" events and experiences that gave and give us joy so they can be given further opportunities for expression.
- Having a chance to reframe our difficulties in light of possibly unexplored gifts and talents.
- Giving ourselves the power to author our own stories, since we—not others—have the "copyright" to our identity.
- Being sensitive to our self-talk (what we mentally tell ourselves about events, people, and ourselves) in order to pick up interpretations and criticism that are not centered in us but in the outside world's set of values and ethics.
- Opening oneself to an array of stories that color our lives but have been thus far underrated (e.g., volunteer work may not be considered "important" because the culture doesn't value it as worthwhile since it is an unpaid activity but after exploration, *we* may see the good we are doing and the joy it may be bringing us).
- Participating in rituals and activities that reinforce and stabilize new, more life-giving identities.

Narrative therapeutic views help us to see more and more of life anew in ways that help our perspective to become more open to possibility. This happens by surfacing assumptions, examining them, and considering alternative views—especially ones developed by *us* and not merely a mimicking of other authority figures (parents, educators, the predominant culture, therapists), no matter how noble their intentions may be.

As Stephen Madigan, author of a small work *Narrative Therapy*, notes,

> From the beginning, a central poststructural tenet of narrative therapy was the idea that we as persons are "multistoried."...Simply stated, narrative therapists took up the position that within the context of therapy, there could be numerous interpretations about persons and problems....And the very interpretations of persons and problems that therapists bring forward are mediated through prevailing ideas held by our culture regarding the specifics of who and what these persons and problems are and what they represent (abnormal/normal, good/bad, worthy/unworthy).

Madigan recognized that people have a reputation with themselves that is very much in line with prevailing ideologies and, in the extreme, prejudices or opinions that have nothing to do with their own values. The goal of narrative therapy is to look at many stories and interpretations in people's lives so they can resist being cast in a way that has possibly held them back. This is exactly what those of us who desire to have a healthy perspective on life and an openness to new views and necessary change *at each stage of life* should also wish for ourselves and put into practice. The fact that this doesn't usually happen with people who have been in our lives for a long period of time was probably the reason for the following quip from Irish playwright, George Bernard Shaw: "The only man who behaved sensibly was my tailor; he took my measure anew every time he saw me, whilst all the rest went on their old measurements and expected them to fit me."

Furthermore, the surprises that exploring our own narrative can provide not only opens us up to expanding our own self-view and horizons, but also sets the stage for entertaining the large questions and puzzles in life. These encounters with "spiritual *koans*" determine our destiny.

3. Traveling Your Own Road to Emmaus

Spiritual Koans, *Letting Go, and Facing Life Afresh!*

Spiritual *koans* are puzzles for which there are no right or wrong answers. They sharpen the edges of different views in life and make us uncomfortable, confused, and sometimes fearful enough to seek to bury them. How we respond to them determines the direction and depth of our faith. If we turn our backs on them, we avoid the spiritual adulthood that contains both the challenges and joys of a life, which is a true pilgrimage. As Plato noted, "We can easily forgive a child who is afraid of the dark; the real tragedy of life is when men are afraid of the light."

Not grappling with a *koan* may help us avoid conflict within, but the price of being simplistic is quite great—not simply for us but also for those whom our lives touch. Moreover, if you were attracted to reading this book, the time would seem ideal to face your *koans*, as is described in the following dialogue between a master and a disciple, shared by Anthony DeMello in his book *One Minute Wisdom*.

"Make a clean break with your past and you will be enlightened," said the Master.

"I am doing that by degrees."

"Growth is achieved by degrees. Enlightenment is instantaneous."

Later he said, "Take the leap! You cannot cross a chasm in little jumps."

Koans may be simple and even involve family-related decisions. Should I give extra attention to an addicted nephew, or should I spend the time with my other nieces and nephews since they don't deserve to be ignored simply because they seem to be on the right track? The *koan* may also be broader in nature, as is the case in the choice of a life partner or mission.

For some, the presidential election in the United States in 2020 also presented as a *koan*. And so, understandingly, some responded to this challenging puzzle by running from it. The Democratic Party's platform that seems to say abortion is all right at any point is hard to embrace—especially if you have witnessed an abortion, especially in the second or third trimester. Behaviors of some others in the Republican Party, which include removing basic environmental protections; making it difficult for the poor to have health insurance; encouraging financial policies that offer the poor and middle-class crumbs and the rich much more, is not in line with Catholic social teaching.

In response, some—including well-known religious figures—seemed to feel they could wave the "right to life" banner as an answer. It certainly is easier to say you wish to protect unborn children than to seek to protect the hidden vulnerable poor or diminish racial hate; or to reach out to the elderly trying to eke out an existence on taxed Social Security benefits; and to show concern about the environment, which is already responsible for the hunger and death of thousands. But hiding behind one position, no matter how important it is, is not a sign of simple faith and spiritual adulthood. Loving one's country is "patriotism" that wants to face and improve what is wrong, whereas simplistic and—dangerous—nationalism seeks to shroud anything unpleasant in a flag. *True* faith is messy.

The easy route is also seen when people say, "*All* lives matter." It is often a response to the Black Lives Matter movement from those who haven't had to face racism and worry about how their children would be treated out on the streets or in business and society.

And so, what is the answer to the spiritual *koan* of elections, for instance since no political party meets all our demands? We must *educate our conscience and decide.* Hiding behind single issues will not prevent the harm we cause that may have even more dire consequences than the position on an issue we have chosen. Though traveling in the same "religious boat" with others who wave the same flag may feel good and comforting, the boat may be going in the wrong direction! This applies as well to those who agree it was all right to publicly refuse communion to public figures they judgmentally felt weren't living up to all the rules of the church.

When we become like those in politics and ministry who yell the loudest when they know the least, we may feel better, but we won't grow. This is costly for both us and those around us. And so, we need to continue to educate our conscience as a way of facing the spiritual *koans* in our own lives. We don't do this to experience pain. We do it because we don't want to miss our lives as a pilgrimage, seeking the truth that contains real joy and peace within it, rather than settling for the simple pleasure and comfort that masquerade as joy and peace. *Koans* are designed to bring us to life and face-to-face with a dynamic, living God. Isn't that what we really want? If it is, we must be willing to *let go* of our fixed positions in order to entertain something even greater—the *good news* and questions that become larger and larger in life.

Lewis H. Lapham observed in an address to a graduating class and their guests at St. John's College in Annapolis, where the curriculum centers on the Great Books:

> When I was your age, I made the mistake of imagining the future as a destination—like Paris or Baltimore or

> the Gobi Desert—and I thought that in the so-called real world the people who ran the place were made of Greek marble or Gothic stone. As I grew older, I began to notice, first to my surprise, and then to my alarm, that the more loudly the Wizards of Oz claimed to know all the answers, the less likely that they knew even a few of the questions. (May 11, 2003)

What Lapham spoke about is letting go of security and certitude in order to be open to more of life and the Spirit than would be possible otherwise.

Letting Go

In his book *Practice Resurrection: A Conversation on Growing Up in Christ*, Eugene Peterson shared a story about a group of friends who decided on taking a mini retreat at a Benedictine monastery known for its hospitality to visitors. Soon after their arrival, the monk in charge of welcoming guests gave them a brief tour, ending with this instruction: "If you find there is anything you need, just ask a brother and he will tell you how to get along without it."

Anthony de Mello once told another brief story to sum up the importance to the spiritual life of the process of "letting go":

> To a disciple who begged for wisdom the Master said, "Try this out: close your eyes and see yourself and every living being thrown off the top of a precipice. Each time you cling to something to stop yourself from falling, understand that it is falling too…"
>
> The disciple tried it out and never was the same again.

These themes of "letting go," "unlearning," and "openness" are present in all religious traditions that seek love and peace at their core. The Dalai Lama, for instance, has often taught that when our mind opens it relaxes and becomes stronger. This requires he says that we seek to move beyond the narrow confines of our self-interest and fear so peace and joy can become our constant companions. However, Nelson Mandela captured it best when he said, "As I walked out the door toward the gate that would lead to my freedom, I knew if I didn't leave my bitterness and hatred behind, I'd still be in prison."

Leaving the comfortable and the familiar, the socially acceptable and the undemanding, requires so much more. The excuses, "holy" excuses, to be sure, abound. While the "enemy" of God is often portrayed as those in the "secular" camp, the dangers are closer to home...so much, much closer, especially when the challenge is to release and *unlearn* as the disciples on the road to Emmaus were called to do, if they were to recognize that Christ was with them.

For Reflection...

"We make our world significant by the courage of our questions, and by the depth of our answers."

– Carl Sagan

True prayer is about many things—but it is most definitely about letting go of insecurity, uncertainty, fear, anger, narcissism, greed, and indifference to important causes highlighted by Jesus. As Archibald Macleish notes, "Religion is at its best when it makes us ask hard questions of ourselves. It is at its worst when it deludes us into thinking we have all the answers for everybody else."

Hearing a "faithful" Catholic say, "I wish Pope Francis would stay out of politics" when Jesus is a model for such behavior, without realizing what he is admitting, is but one example. Having religious leaders endorse civic leaders whose only claim to Christian fame is to be against abortion while they turn a blind eye to other evils is another. But, before we distance ourselves from them, among the spiritual questions that this book poses are: What psychological factors are keeping *us* from recognizing our own hesitancy to embrace pure love and truth...to meet God? What should *our* response be to God's call to spiritual intimacy in such tough or confusing times?

Contemplative, Trappist monk, and spiritual writer Thomas Merton was intrigued by the philosopher Jaspers's comment that life is both difficult and possible. He recognized that we don't want to see this and as a result we divide it and feel that life is either easy or impossible. The same can be said of the spiritual life: it is both possible...*and* not easy, although simple if we embrace pure love and truth. And that is the focus and challenge of this book: to explore the psychological perils of spiritual intimacy. This intimacy will bring great joy but requires a complete letting go of other "idols" and "gods" even if they be religion, "the church" as certain people term it, or our own scriptural interpretations. Spiritual intimacy requires a willingness to entertain a full-faced encountering of the truth.

This doesn't mean that we will not have issues, questions, or stumble on the road to such an intimacy. As was noted, Merton indicated that "with deep faith comes deep doubt so give up the business of suppressing doubt." But it does mean we have to stop fooling ourselves. Yet, letting go of our long-held opinions isn't always easy—especially if they are so ingrained that we don't even appreciate that we should examine them periodically.

Chinese philosopher Lao Tzu once said, "The usefulness of the cup is its emptiness." In speaking with many psychotherapists, spiritual directors, mentors, or coaches, there are questions they wished they could or would have asked the persons who came to them for help or guidance. Surprisingly, many of them are almost all about one thing: *letting go*.

Maybe those questions weren't asked because in pacing the session, they didn't seem appropriate. Possibly as they walked with persons on a turn in their psychological or spiritual journey, they felt the question would ask too much—and maybe that was true at the time. Or, in their *own* lives as helpers, the questions may not have surfaced because they also were afraid of where they might lead for the individual. No matter what the reason, the end result is the same: less inner freedom and a failure to fully fathom the amazing paradox of letting go in order to meet God and life in new ways: *metanoia*.

When people speak of "releasing" or "letting go," it is often in reference to a specific desire, possession, or relationship. But while jettisoning a particular attachment can be the source of new inner "lightness," letting go is so much more than that. What this spirit offers can be an almost indescribable gift *if* it is fully understood and becomes the cornerstone of an overall attitude of freedom that is constantly renewed and experienced—especially in one's relationship with God.

We experience relief when we release our grasp—even of something that may initially have been beneficial or practical. When the timing is right, the movement toward new freedom is wonderful. But to be honest and realistic, such freedom is often short-lived. The room swept clean no longer remains that way. The empty space that originally opened up new opportunities for creativity, compassion, wisdom, and the experience of God in our lives soon starts to fill up again. It need not be with something bad or addictive, but it fills us nonetheless; life no longer has the sense of the fresh possibility that it did for a while.

Unfortunately, the resulting harm we often experience is not usually recognized for some time. And, when it is finally discovered, we experience a sense of self-betrayal or remorse. This feeling may even lead us to think, "I am back where I started—or even further back. What's the use!"

On the other hand, when there is a sense of openness to nurturing an attitude of releasing or letting go, even when grasping becomes temporarily prevalent again, all is not lost. There is at least an appreciation of the fact that our new free space has slowly and quietly become contaminated again. This should not be surprising because habit (or the influences from the past and the society in which one lives) can be very persuasive. Inner freedom cannot permanently be maintained. It is also why daily meditation—even for a few moments because regularity is more important than only occasional longer periods—is not a nicety. It is necessary for a graced perspective on life, *our* life. Otherwise, the only time when we will have a true perspective on life and what is essential will be when someone dies or there is illness or loss is experienced. How foolish it is to live like this. So much is lost or overlooked; so many graced gifts remain unopened.

Still, the good news is that, when we are mindful of the natural tendency to retreat to the familiar, a reservoir of integrity always remains within us that values both honesty and clarity. Paradoxically, this awareness of having pulled back again can seed an even more intense desire to practice letting go anew—maybe this time with greater wisdom concerning the challenges all of us face.

For Reflection...

"To dare is to lose one's footing momentarily.
Not to dare is to lose oneself."

– Søren Kierkegaard

And so, when new idols and fears appear, even though they may be temporarily bowed to, the spiritual pilgrimage to experiencing life and God more directly and fully never totally ceases again. The rewards of avoiding grasping and ego tightfistedness are experienced more quickly. The loosening of our psychological grip and being able to smile at the amount of peace and joy during the day is felt. Yes, *deeply* felt. Then everything becomes easier because the art of letting go is experienced and honored more often—not because it should be, but because to us it simply makes sense to do so.

For this to happen, knowledge, discipline, and commitment to enhance our outlook and practice with respect to opening ourselves up to life are essential companions. And so, with this reality before us, as a way to dispel any notion of spiritual or psychological romanticism about the process being easy, automatic, or magical, we need to reflect or journal on letting go and touching the holy afresh.

These mental and spiritual "companions" are designed to put our own, as well as the experience of others (both their successes and failures), at our disposal. Our own reflections can track the ongoing unfolding of our own lives, since this is a simple but powerful way to learn from personal experiences and reactions.

Utilizing such information helps us to appreciate and record personal breakthroughs and occurrence of possibly unnecessary mistakes. In the development of our own reflections on inner freedom, a search is immediately undertaken for what works best, given our unique background, circumstances, personality style, and current beliefs. By unearthing this information, we can begin to more intentionally enjoy the pilgrimage toward greater inner freedom to make new space for the *experience* of, and relationship with, God. We can also see that attending to flowing with life, rather than merely drifting, is such an intriguing and rewarding daily endeavor, in and of itself. Even when it is difficult and we stumble, we learn from these encounters. There can be an ultimate satisfaction even in failure when alone-time is part of our lives and approached in a way that opens us up rather than leads us to self-blame, projection of our difficulties onto others, or discouragement when what we want doesn't happen on our timeline.

Spiritual Freshness

Being "born again" means many things to many people but most would agree that it is synonymous with being given a fresh start in life. One of the major fruits of facing our *koans* and "letting go" is a sense of freshness about life—being born from above. We recognize that change is a constant in life. Rather than being mired in past events and connections (even if they were good at the time) or reading a menu of fantasies or desires for the future, we can experience the present fully. In doing this, we can recognize that in many ways the past was sacred, and the future will be holy. But it is only in the "now" that the living, dynamic God is encountered.

To appreciate this, a person who *lives* with spiritual wisdom always has a self-definition of being a learner and a student, beginning anew again and again. And so, there is no final spiritual graduation. The recognition, instead, is that life will repeatedly knock us off our spiritual or religious positions, which is not an imposition but a reaffirmation. Unless we freshly face life and our appreciation of God in a yet deeper way, our approach is tantamount to idol worship of our past images. Yet, this is not easy to remember. Falling prey to other values and goals in life is so easy and is reinforced by society, unless someone or something steps in. As Erling Kagge in his book *Silence in the Age of Noise* notes,

> Questions and answers, questions, and answers. Wonder is the very engine of life. But my children are thirteen, sixteen, and nineteen years old and wonder less and less; if they still wonder at anything, they quickly pull out their smartphones to find the answer. They are still curious, but their faces are not as childish, more adult, and their heads are now filled with more ambitions than questions.

Or, in the words of John of the Cross with respect to letting go and being open:

> We are not talking here about giving up things, because that does not strip the soul if her affective drive remains set on them. We are talking about stripping away the craving for gratification (*gusto, apetito*) in those things. That is what leaves the person free and empty in their regard, even though she still owns them. Because it is not the things of this world that take up space in the person or do her harm....No, it is the will and the hunger for them that dwell inside her.

In another place, John would go on to say that a choice for God would truly allow him to take flight rather than be tied down by the wrong or lesser desires.

When Zen sage, Shunryu Suzuki was admiring a classic tea bowl, his mentor passed by and said to him, "Don't commit adultery!" In saying this, he wasn't indicating that he shouldn't appreciate beautiful things but just that he shouldn't become attached or caught by them. To experience a sense of letting go and freshness, at times we must also be willing to face not simply painful questions about life, meaning, and God, but also ones like the following about ourselves:

- What are my primary signature strengths, talents, and virtues? Under what circumstances do they become distorted, buried, or exaggerated?
- What are the comments made about me that I love or hate and why do I feel I react this way?
- What behavior in myself and others do I find abhorrent? In addition to their being negative, what is the reason they *especially* bother me?
- What type of people am I particularly drawn to and who actually represents those type of individuals in my life now?
- Who in my life do I not want to spend time with and what are the reasons for this?

As part of the letting go process, darkness is experienced at times. When it does occur, there are actually some positive sides to this unwanted spiritual territory that may arise. They include:

- More profound self-understanding due to learning about our many gifts—including, *especially*, the "minor" ones that have gone unnoticed or are little experienced and honored *until* we are going through a tough time and need them.

- Clearer sense of our vulnerabilities and a desire to understand, rather than run away from them.
- Sense of inner peace that doesn't require the approval of others or achieving success or finding what we believe to be security.
- Deeper awareness of our motivations and personality style under pressure or when anxious.
- Broader array of interpersonal skills developed when our usual ones aren't effective.
- Greater appreciation of the fact that seeking to be successful is not as important as learning from those times when we are not.

Yet, for this to happen we must position ourselves to both let go and be open to receiving new and different ways of psychologically viewing life, ourselves, and God. To reach this place, we must have courage, patience, solitude, a willingness to sit in silence, and to be wrapped in gratitude without wanting to "accomplish" something. "Simply" being attentive with a sense of trust is the attitude needed.

Such welcoming of "spiritual freshness" allows us to sit beside our fears, anxieties, and hopes in a new way. Instead of being caught in a cocoon of self-talk, we stop speaking to ourselves, relax, and "just sit" while allowing the *Teacher* to appear in the present moment. It is a true case of what existential philosopher and Christian theologian Paul Tillich would refer to as "ecstatic reasoning," where we are desirous of connecting the immediate with the ultimate.

For Reflection...

"There is always light, if only we're brave enough to see it. If only we're brave enough to be it."

– Amanda Gorman
Youngest Poet Laureate in US History

Setting aside time for quiet meditative periods is one important step in setting the stage for this reality to become possible. Slowly, if we remain intrigued about what may come up, our honesty will become more frequent and, like Nathaniel, whom Jesus spotted under a tree and warmly greeted, we will seek to become persons without guile who can purify the "psychological and spiritual air" for ourselves and others. In addition, there will be a greater tendency to have low expectations and high hopes and less concern about how we are coming across to others and our own ego. Pema Chödrön wrote in her famous work *When Things Fall Apart*, "Being preoccupied with our self-image [is] like coming upon a tree of singing birds while wearing ear plugs."

In addition, quiet meditation and a desire for spiritual freshness will be marked by our enjoying and relaxing with life *as it is*, rather than holding onto the fiction we wish were the case. In this way, we will not demand that life be a certain way as a price for our happiness. Finally, our minds will no longer be dominated with the world's values that are of little importance, but rather will embrace the great values, and chief among them the love that Jesus and other spiritual figures spoke about and modeled for us.

Valuing "letting go" also enables us to begin to see that self-absorption—overconcern about what others think, our public image and fame—are actually cloaks we put over the luminous experiences of directly encountering life as it unfolds.

After all, how can we open the door to epiphanies and awe if we can't even see that the opening is there because of our self-preoccupation? We need space and time for this. As Zena Hitz in her work *Lost in Thought* notes, "The inwardness of the mind at leisure unlocks the dignity that is so often denied by social life and social circumstances." She sees as well that "an inner life is not...solitary self-involvement" but actually a place where we can invite "the comradeship of good thoughts." The letting go experience and the desire for an apophatic (emptying) space is a testament to the belief in Jesuit theologian Karl Rahner's comment that "the Christian of the future will be a mystic or he or she will not exist at all." Nowhere is this a more apt understanding of the process and necessity of letting go and welcoming the new than in the case when we experience trauma, great stress, and a serious sense of darkness in our lives.

Posttraumatic Growth (PTG) and the Spirituality of Suffering

One of the greatest spiritual *koans* is trauma. When persons are physically attacked in war or sexually assaulted, they are certainly emotionally and spiritually violated as well. Death of a loved one and a loss of one's means of financial support can also produce a deep sense of loss and of personal meaning, similar to boundary violations and violence, and can be quite traumatic as well.

Some people experience great trauma and loss in life, and this must be respected as both significant and unique. However, all of us encounter some level of trauma and loss and it may cause all types of difficulties. They can range from problems with intimacy and trust to self-destructive behavior and weight problems (anorexia or obesity), all the way to drug and alcohol abuse.

In studying how healing is possible the "spirituality of suffering" has long posed and reflected upon such questions as:

- Why does God permit horrible events to happen?
- I thought God said that I would not be alone when I walked through the valley of darkness—well, where was God when I was raped or tortured?
- My spouse was such a good person. Why did this wonderful individual die so young while so many who behave awfully are permitted to live?

However, along with the spirituality of suffering, healing, and recovery, in which the person seeks to find meaning and added comfort for self and others who face similar difficulties, the mental health profession has much more recently explored posttraumatic growth (PTG) from a psychological perspective. Its tenet is that if we remain honest as to the horror of the trauma or loss, on the one hand, and are open to where it may take us, on the other, something amazing might happen. We may grow and deepen in ways that would not have happened had the trauma, serious stress, or dramatic loss *not happened in the first place.* The reality remains that most persons would trade PTG for the event not having happened. Yet, since it did happen, the chance for something good (spiritual healing and new personal depth as a person) should be honored. To increase the possibility of this happening, the gift of psychological knowledge about the process of PTG can help us navigate the perils involved.

Initially, an array of negative emotions occurs as part of truly acknowledging what has happened. This is also part of the grieving process and includes sadness, loneliness, guilt, shame, regret, anxiety, anger, depression, and even despair. There is a sense of permanency about a change and irrevocable loss that has happened in one's life. What makes the person feel worse is also a sense of helplessness and even panic that may cause regression. In response, there may be a temptation in some to excuse, minimize, deny, or spiritually romanticize what has happened.

For Reflection...

"I am an old man full of love. I am a man of faith.
But faith is not necessarily,
or not soon, a resting place. Faith puts you
out on a wide river in a little boat,
in the fog, in the dark."

– Jayber Crow

That the seeds of such grief and negative emotions may also be the seeds of new life doesn't deny the loss or trauma but does offers portals to new understanding and possibilities that couldn't have arisen before. The shock to one's previous sense of meaning and structure of life and outlook leads to a total reevaluation of how and why one has lived in a particular way up to this point. The basic assumptions about life are shattered.

From a psychological perspective, the person begins to realize more profoundly what has happened and, in accepting the reality at some point, appreciates that while the trauma is real, it doesn't represent their whole past, present, or future life. This acceptance begins to break up what was a complete psychologically dark sky into a series of "emotional clouds" that are real but no longer completely overwhelming. From a spiritual vantage point, the previous religious sense of God and life is crushed, or at least goes through a significant disassembling, which opens up the possibility of an even deeper, more mature, and compassionate sense of faith and the divine. For instance, a more sensitive awareness of the crucifixion as well as an appreciation of God walking *alongside* me may become more powerful and vivid. Compassion for others' suffering and feeling a greater solidarity with them in heartfelt ways not possible before also may happen.

Psychologically, the ability is there to care for oneself and others in new, nurturing ways. Simple encounters with music, nature, and comforting events may also evolve and be honored in a vastly vibrant way. In turn, the ability to honor others' rage and depression, as well as one's own, often increases. A person at this point in the healing process and road to PTG may remark how freeing it is now to express negative emotions they didn't feel comfortable sharing in the past. They also begin to have greater insight into how far they have come in the time since the trauma or significant, stressful event.

To enable this, both therapists and spiritual guides alike must be patient and provide an accepting and safe environment, so the person coming to them can express any emotion—even anger at God—without fearing they are doing something wrong. With such modeling by mentors and counselors, the person can feel more open with themselves and God. God is no longer too big or too fragile to hear the request that the cup be passed on or the anger that this fate has dealt to them.

Also, with the assumptions one may have lived by being shattered, an appreciation for life and others, and the emergence of new, more creative coping skills may occur. And so, one's self-view may change, interpersonal style may alter, and priorities may be shuffled. If this doesn't happen, rumination may occur about why the event happened until one's perspective on life can be revised. In addition, all of this alters how one meets difficulties in the future, whether their own or other people's.

Two of the key elements in PTG occurring are patience and timing. In ourselves and others, we need to be open to the possibilities dark times bring us but not push ourselves or people who turn to us after a trauma. Otherwise, guilt and pressure to "get better," "let go," or "deepen" may inadvertently result. On the other hand, without an openness to positive change, new possibilities might be missed. As in meditation and contemplation, a sense of intrigue is the middle ground. So if or when something surprisingly positive happens amidst the sadness, anger, and grief, it is honored. In the words of French existentialist Albert Camus, "In the depths of winter, I finally learned that within me lay an invincible summer"; this is the outcome that all must be open to but not forced. Camus's words also acknowledge that not only do trauma and stress lead to negative results...they also can produce awe-filled positive change. Suffering and loss need not be the final words psychologically or spiritually. Instead, they may be a dramatic beginning for good. In the words of another famous survivor—this time of a Nazi concentration camp—psychiatrist Victor Frankl in his classic work, *Man's Search for Inner Meaning*, writes, "To live is to suffer, to survive is to find meaning in the suffering."

Part of the healing process is to understand what went wrong. But just as important, the culmination of the healing process for many, is to ask, what am I learning about life that is paradoxically life-giving to me and others because of this horrible event? Much will be determined by the personality of the person, details of the negative event(s), how and to whom the person is able to self-disclose, religious-cultural-familial influences, and how the distress is handled. All of this will impact assumptions and beliefs about the world—what they were and what they might develop into now. In essence, new forms of meaning-making will need to occur.

Much has now been written on PTG for both psychotherapists and a general audience. In one of these books by Werdel and Wicks, a summative statement made is:

> When we fall, do we get up? And if we get up, do we get to an up experience that is cognitively and emotionally different than where we were before we and our physical and assumptive worlds fell down? And within this sense of newness is there anything positive? Or is it merely negative or neutral? These are the fundamental questions of the work of stress and growth.
>
> Posttraumatic growth advocates do not presume in any way that new and different experiences, understandings, or perspectives are always positive, but sometimes pieces of them are. Accordingly, the study of posttraumatic growth is not a comparison of pre-and post-lives in the sense that one is better or worse. Instead, it is the study of coming to terms and accepting what is different and about questioning the piece or pieces that are different and determining if they have intrinsically positive qualities that are worthy of being honored for what they are. When these qualities are honored, amazing results become truly possible.

There is also a great deal written on the spirituality of suffering that predates what is written on PTG by a significant time period. In many ways, spiritual themes produce interest in psychological circles to find the human component or research results to determine not simply the validity of something, but also how mental health can support the goals that spirituality and theology set out. Again, from Werdel and Wicks' *A Primer on Posttraumatic Growth*:

> The construal of human suffering from a Christian faith perspective provides significance to the experience. Suffering is not isolated and pointless. Suffering, like all life events, is construed in terms of one's relationship to Jesus (Roberts, 2007). Suffering is a meaning-filled component that can be grist for the mill of living the spiritual life if people's religious convictions are able to integrate it (Hauser, 1994). If integrated in a mature way, faith can continue the emotional experience of suffering as a useful way to acknowledge and deepen their personal relationship with God. People may, for example, come to realize that they are in a privileged context (Harrington, 2000), sharing parallel experiences with their god. From a Christian perspective, they may find more meaning in personal relationships and more purpose in life by feeling a deeper connection with God.
>
> So then while human suffering can slam its victim against a solid wall of evil, according to certain Christian apologists, so too can it also transform its victims into some of the most beautiful of persons (Liderbach, 1992). From this point of view, the Christian faith does not seek struggle, but it acknowledges that it exists and so uses it, as it does all else, to form a deeper relationship with God through the self and with God through others. In this faith tradition, it is interesting that just as in the scientific process of posttraumatic growth, the trauma, the stress, and the suffering are allowed to remain intrinsically negative while also allowed to be the fulcrum and impetus for new, possibly amazing, growth.

A religious belief system and faith tradition have the possibility of helping us make meaning of difficult, even traumatic, times; using psychology as a help only adds to the chance this process will be beneficial. With spirituality to call us forth, a faith to support us, and sound psychology to help us plow the rocky fields of PTG and to take the most mature fork in the road when faced with the *koans* in life, much good can result. And such outcomes not only stand to benefit us, but also will naturally have the outgrowth of inspiring others to live full, compassionate, meaningful, and rewarding lives as well.

The world is a stage…how we walk, or even dance, on it is dramatically different for each person. Stories continue to abound with helpers as they seek to keep afloat while they stand with others suffering and dying. One of the caregivers from Aleppo who came to a workshop in Lebanon on maintaining resilience, shared that a young girl once asked him, "Why am I losing the best years of my life? Why am I not like the rest of the girls in the world? Why do I not have the right to live fully my youth? Is this God's will? Why does he not answer our prayers and our pleas? In spite of our trust in him, we do not see the end of the tunnel…"

The brother then added, "What answer can I give her and to many other young persons? I listen to them, I support them, I try to seek to stutter words of trust and of faith. This is not always easy."

Yet, darkness need not be the final word. A pastoral counseling student, who was known for her good spirit and optimism in her graduate program, wrote a final paper that included her biography. Knowing her to be a person of great hope and resilience, the professor admitted that he was dumbfounded after reading it. He was astounded so much so that he actually approached her and asked, "Is what you wrote about your life true?" She was caught off-guard by the question, as one might expect, and replied, "Why, of *course*!"

He said, "I read that your husband died early in the marriage, leaving you with two sons to raise. The older of the two died in a car crash and the younger committed suicide years later, and yet I don't exaggerate that despite the multiple tragedies you have experienced, you are a beacon of hope for the other students. I also expect you will be that for those you counsel and your colleagues as well going forward. How did this happen given all you have been through?"

She responded, "Well, it was all horrible, tragic, and very hard. *Very* hard. However, I eventually realized that I had a choice. I could let it psychologically bury me or I could let it soften my soul and help me honor the rest of my life and aid others who have been through so much to do the same."

Understanding posttraumatic growth and the spirituality of suffering is all about choices and the support we need to make the best ones in—even in, *especially* in—the darkness. Yet, to do so, we need to honor the psychological resistances we have in facing and embracing spiritual wisdom. It is not easy to be clear, especially in a world that often pulls us in directions that are not helpful, and toward attitudes that are certainly not of God.

4. Overcoming Psychological Resistance to Spiritual Wisdom

Clarity, Critical Thinking, Discernment, and Alone-Time

In bringing to the fore our desire to remove blocks to our relationship with truth, we must recognize that the natural movement in us is to *resist* because of the discomfort it might cause at times. Knowing this, John Sanford is his classic work, *Healing and Wholeness*, writes,

> Deep inside each organism is something that knows what that organism's true nature and life goal is. It is as though there is within each person an inner center that knows what constitutes health. If our conscious personality becomes related to the inner center, the whole person may begin to emerge, though this may not bring either peace or social adaptation, but conflict and stress.... The movement toward health may look more like a crucifixion than adaptation or peace of mind.

One of the sure signs of psychological resistance to encountering the truth about oneself is a sense of vagueness. Clarity, on the other hand, cuts through the defenses of "suppression" and "repression" (unconscious and conscious forgetting). It is for this reason that therapists and spiritual directors often ask for illustrations when a person coming to see them makes a broad statement or expresses an overriding strong feeling about some person or situation.

A theological reflection, at the end of each day, is built on such a search for clarity as well. Persons undertaking such a process, as a matter of course:

- Look at the objective geography of the day—*what* happened?
- Image being back in the events in order to examine the subjective responses experienced—how did I *feel* and *react*?
- Determine the cognitions (ways of thinking, perceiving, and understanding) about the events and interactions that led to the resultant feelings and actions.
- Finally, given the outcome of doing this, examine their own spirituality, theology, and appreciation of Sacred Scripture to see what insights can be gleaned.

Then ask: What needs to be unlearned and newly learned now to enliven one's outlook, subsequent behavior, and personal theology and spirituality? Taking this all together, the theological reflection is designed to lead to new dynamic ways of acting and experiencing self, situations, others, and God.

As part of this psychological and spiritual journey, a number of questions naturally arise, including:

- What is the overall generative style I have in interacting with others and what are some of the lesser talents and gifts I should be enhancing in order to enjoy myself and be more compassionate with others?

- Under what circumstances do I "psychologically trip over" my God-given style and become defensive or extreme in my response?
- What comments do I dislike being made about me and what are the reasons such evaluations particularly upset me?
- Accordingly, what type of persons do I gravitate toward or away from in life? How do I understand such reactions on my part?
- What makes me most angry, anxious, stressed or, on the other hand, relaxed, affirmed, and enlightened?

Such a desire spiritually to have greater clarity about life and self, crosses various religious traditions. For instance, in a dialogue from the book *Bones of the Master* by Crane, between a nonbeliever and a Chinese Buddhist (Chan) master, the nonbeliever remarks positively on the monk's state of mind to which the master responds,

"Everything is the same. Just concentration."

The nonbeliever then admits, "I think I need to get some of this concentration."

The Chan master simply replies simply and directly, "You need very much. Good for your life."

Critical Thinking

In philosophy, education, and psychology, the search for clarity and truth involves applying the skills associated with *critical thinking*, including:

- A willingness to be open to new knowledge and unlearn preconceived notions that may have been helpful at one point in life but aren't now.

- Basing one's position on observations, fact gathering, analyzing, conceptualizing, and willingness to look at alternative explanations.
- Intellectually disciplined and systematically applied findings.

The critical thinking process can lead to greater clarity with the belief that almost any issue or person can be faced because we are able to feel the biblical injunction, "Be not afraid." This, in turn, provides a milieu within which to ask ourselves questions to gain greater clarity, such as:

- Am I willing to deal with uncertainties and ambiguities, and live with the questions rather than seeking closure and answers?
- What are the ways I seek new knowledge rather than enclose myself in current beliefs during times of change and potential growth?
- How do I face doubt and the need for "unlearning" as a way to meet life when it becomes different at each stage, as does a dynamic God?
- What is my reaction to the following statement by the Reverend Martin Luther King Jr.? "The ultimate measure of a man is not where he stands in moments of comfort and convenience, but where he stands at times of challenge and controversy. The true neighbor will risk his position, his prestige, and even his life for the welfare of others."

And so, just as occurs in a mentoring, spiritual direction, or counseling session, the goal of clarity for ourselves is sought in a number of ways through self-reflection. To enhance this process, we seek to elaborate and find illustrations, as well as question the accuracy of our thinking and logic when examining our feelings and behavior. This leads to greater accuracy and personal depth as a person, as well as greater understanding and knowledge of ourselves, others, God, and the situations we encounter. We also appreciate the often-unrecognized power of interpretations, assumptions, implications, and precision. This leads us to recognize more quickly and completely how the voices of culture and a desire for success and competitiveness, financial prosperity, as well as security and certainty, can drown out the voice of God.

True critical thinking and spiritual discernment may not lead to comfort, but they do produce long-lasting peace and joy and an ongoing desire for clarity. Surrounding ourselves with like-minded, searching souls, and at least a few wisdom figures, helps in our journey to embrace truth.

For Reflection...

"When you are fooled by something else, the damage will not be so big. But when you are fooled by yourself, it is fatal. No more medicine."

– Shunryu Suzuki

What we must also recognize is that critical thinking's counterpart is *discernment*. In this spiritual process, we reflect on our external encounters and interior experiences to determine or sort out if we are welcoming or avoiding a "call" to see the truth about what God is telling us. While discernment doesn't deny the role of God's grace in the process, neither does it underplay our role in seeking clarity as to whether our motivations and responses are predominantly from God or from something or someone else. Family, peers, society, career, upbringing, and our ego all are voices that can support our spiritual journey or become louder than the voice of God. Discernment is also not a once-and-for-all process. As Farnham, Gill, McLean, and Word image in their book *Listening Hearts*, "Discernment can be like driving an automobile at night: the headlights cast only enough light for us to see the next bit of road immediately in front of us." In other words, in seeking truth through the process of discernment in our psychological effort to gain clarity, we seek to find the next step we need to take. Once that is done, new information to discern following steps becomes more evident. In the process, we will make mistakes, and if we face them correctly, they will teach us as well.

Supporting the discernment process is time spent with Sacred Scripture, a willingness to face uncertainty, the ability to let go and unlearn, as well as a basic trust in God. At times, overconfidence and insecurity will occur. By being sensitive to their appearance, we can then remember the need for humility, on the one hand, and reasonable self-confidence and perseverance, on the other.

Honoring Psychological Resistances to Clarity, Growth, and Change

In support of being like Nathaniel, a person without guile, especially favorably cited by Jesus, and seeking to have purity of heart, psychology suggests we recognize and take efforts to remove psychological defenses to seeing more clearly our role in avoiding insight. When we abandon old habits and styles that no longer apply and address unexamined negative beliefs, there is a greater chance that autonomy (our will) and theonomy (God's will) will become more integrated, so we have greater freedom in life. Psychological defenses can also be "emotionally expensive." They prevent us from taking reasonable risks to encounter the living God—even when we feel we are doing the opposite!

To soften up these areas, Wicks in his book *Simple Changes* provides "several rediscovery caveats to help reduce the resistance to letting go" of current blocks to clarity and change:

1. Anything discovered does not have to be changed immediately.
2. No area should be condemned as holding on—just neutrally observed as if it were happening to someone else.
3. No area should be defended—no one is criticizing or attacking, just observing where energy is being spent.
4. Observations—even disturbing ones—should be embraced as a wonderful treasure trove of information.
5. After each period of observation, the areas of concern should be written down, so some record is kept of their discovery.

We can see we are *not* doing this when we are involved in being judgmental, projecting the blame onto others, and being overly perfectionistic without appreciating God's love for us or the presence of Grace. Strong feelings can be "psychological blinking lights" that we are anxious, fearful, or desirous of running away from truth. When this happens, as was noted in *Simple Changes*, we can recall the caveats just mentioned as a way to "make friends with our resistances," because if we take them on directly and immediately, we will often become discouraged and fail.

For Reflection...

"'It's true what you say, Reine-Marie,' said Claude. 'People believe what they want to believe. Beginning with their own lies.'"

– Louise Penny, *All the Devils Are Here: A Novel*

We can recognize we are becoming freer and letting go more often, when having a sense of curiosity and intrigue about both our gifts and growing edges becomes more the norm for our attitude toward seeking more of the truth about ourselves. Our time in silence and solitude helps to soften our souls and make us more generous and open, rather than self-serving, rigid, and fearful of new experiences (be they seen as "negative" or "positive") that can invite us to become awake and mindful. Finally, in the search to be clearer, we also allow the whole discernment and self-awareness process to rest more lightly instead of being the stage on which we obsessively and intensely seek to figure out and control our lives. As a result, we need to tease ourselves more often when we get too wrapped up in finding the truth and seeking God. In this way, we can avoid catastrophizing life, forgetting Grace and God's involvement in the process, or developing unrealistic expectations for our own role in the process.

The overall goal is to be an "enthusiastic listener" to all of our thoughts, perceptions, and ways of understanding, as well as to the emotions and style of behavior they produce. Honest information gathering (without censoring or excusing certain thoughts or behaviors) can reduce resistance to growth and change so as to welcome the Spirit...Truth. When the process becomes uncomfortable or confusing, as it certainly will at different points, this is not a cause for discouragement. Instead, it is a call that we may need someone wiser and holier to walk with us through this emotional and spiritual night.

When all else fails, reflecting on and praying about the theme of *impermanence* will often release us from being imprisoned in the moment by our past and by anxiety about the future. Such a meditation may be about someone else. Mary Oliver, in reflecting on the loss of a dear friend, shared that she was ready to send her some roses that she picked for her when she suddenly heard that she had died. In her own words, she suddenly knew that nothing she would send to her dear friend could arrive in time anymore. It can also be about us as we recognize how fast the time has gone in our lives and how little of it is left.

Finally, there are some basic truths worth knowing from the psychology of defensiveness and resistance to change that will help us to have low expectations and high hopes that if we approach discernment humbly and faithfully, we will be fine. They include:

- None of us is totally free. The question is, where are these resistances to change?
- Discouragement is natural at times as we seek to know ourselves better, but if these moments teach us that clarity must be balanced by gentleness and a greater awareness of God's love, they too can be a support for our search.
- Every emotion we have is tied to our cognitions (ways of thinking, perceiving, and understanding) and include both immature and mature reasons for believing what is good and evil.

Nowhere are the above recognized more clearly that in experiences of alone-time, where we are called to go deeper. Once again, to quote the poet Rumi:

> Maybe you are searching among the branches, for what only appears in the roots.

Time spent in silence and solitude while wrapped in gratitude for God is one of the most powerful ways to sense the presence (and absence) of God through the Spirit (Truth) in our lives. Yet, since the encounter with God in alone-time is both beautiful and causes resistance, it is worth addressing.

The Gifts and Surprising Challenges of Alone-Time

People sit in silence, solitude, and wrapped in gratitude, as a way of finding God and solid psychological grounding in their lives. And so, sitting quietly, possibly alone, with an empty mind and a spirit of openness and trust, can open the door to peace, as well as the inner turmoil that may actually be a portal to a deeper relationship with God. In light of this, silence and solitude and being wrapped in gratitude before God are not luxuries for the select. They represent psychological and spiritual "gates" that we would all do well to walk through.

Contemplation frees us for truth, not a partial encounter with reality. If we don't resist seeing things as they are, as we are, freedom is the fruit. In doing so, we slowly open ourselves to almost natural change for the good. As the Zen saying, previously shared, goes: Face reality and unwilled change will take place. Moreover, one of the main graces of contemplation also impacts others around us: namely, we increase the chance that we will become persons, like Nathaniel, without guile who can purify the "psychological and spiritual air" for those around us. It also sets the stage for us to *experience* life and God in simple, powerful ways. As Thomas Merton notes,

> When your tongue is silent, you can rest in the silence of the forest. When your imagination is silent, the forest speaks to you. It tells you of its unreality and of the Reality of God. But when your mind is silent, then the forest suddenly becomes magnificently real and blazes transparently with the Reality of God.

Contemplation, in particular, provides us with the gift of greater clarity by offering us the room to let thoughts rise out of the preconscious that we have submerged for some reason. In allowing this to occur, humility becomes more possible since we see our foibles, fears, and the games we play on behalf of entitlement, greed, cowardice, and avoiding vulnerability. We also begin to learn to have less dependence on the reinforcement of others and can become more in tune with change and accept loss more readily. Our inner fire is protected as we have a chance to move away from the compulsive activities of existence so we can appreciate life and become more in tune with the voice of God over the other voices constantly calling for our attention. Walking with God is the oldest form of prayer described in Sacred Scripture.

For Reflection...

"Prayer requires education, training, reflection, contemplation. It is not enough to join others; it is necessary to build a sanctuary within, brick by brick, instants of meditation, moments of devotion. This is particularly true in an age when overwhelming forces seem to conspire at destroying our ability to pray."

– Abraham Joshua Heschel

With contemplation we reenter that garden with a sense of hope and an understanding from Jesus that we are loved. This can then impact our daily outlook significantly in that we don't need a dramatic revelation to know God is present. A smile of an older person, the laughter of a child, a flower blossoming all become "messages from heaven" because we are now more aware, empty, free, and grateful. And this all becomes possible not because we have achieved something but because we have offered space for Grace, for God. In the word of John of the Cross, "nada," we have gotten out of the way so we can experience the Way.

In *Inner Christianity*, Richard Smoley writes,

> When the turbulence of the mind and emotions have subsided, consciousness becomes still and clear, and the presence of God can be felt. Although, as we are constantly reminded, God is everywhere, we are rarely aware of this fact because our mental agitation makes it impossible to experience his presence. Practically all techniques of prayer and meditation are aimed at stilling the mind so that the Absolute can be made manifest in us.

Yet, despite the wonderful possibilities of contemplation, time for it isn't prioritized in many people's schedule. Although the reason proffered for this is that life is so busy, this is rarely the case. We always seem to have time for what we want to do, as is the case in the following story of an interaction between psychotherapists:

> *A psychologist shared with one of his colleagues that after he graduated, one of his first patients was a physician with one of the busiest practices in the city. The reason he wanted to see him was that he was having an extramarital*

affair. He said to his friend that at the time he gave the patient a Freudian analysis of his actions.

"What would you tell him now," the other psychotherapist asked.

"Instead, I would ask him, 'Where do you get the time?!'" and they both laughed.

No matter how involved we are, we always seem to find time for what we want to do. And so, the reason for not praying because one is too busy is in most cases not true. As Steven Covey once noted in a lecture, "Don't simply prioritize your schedule. Schedule your priorities." To this, we can add, recognize the many resistances to sitting in silence as a way of appreciating why we would undermine a prayer form that most of us claim we want at the heart of our lives so we can live with greater clarity, meaning, and closeness to God.

One of the core reasons we avoid contemplation is that when we are silent, we create a vacuum in the present, and as all of us learned in high school science class, nature abhors physical vacuums so seeks to fill them. The same can be said with respect to the psychological emptiness that is created when we spiritually seek to be alone with God. The reaction of our ego is to fill the vacuum in our consciousness. As a result, the "preconscious," those areas just beyond our awareness (or from a cognitive-behavioral perspective, our unexamined ways of thinking, perceiving, and understanding our behavior and the world around us) rise up to the surface and fill our mental void.

When this occurs, we are left facing our anxieties, fears, shame, doubt, and even possible questions about God's actual existence, that lie just below our surface awareness. The response that would help us with this is neither to try to suppress these unwanted thoughts, feelings, and memories nor to entertain them. Instead, they need to be allowed to move by us like a boat on a river, which we take note of but don't concentrate on. If the same ones keep floating by, they can simply be put into the hands of God.

In either case, there are great benefits if we don't psychologically run away from the experience. First, it will allow us to see the negative thoughts, misunderstandings, erroneous beliefs, and unhelpful messages we have received from others that lie just beyond our normal level of awareness. This is important because the only memory or mental driving force that will hurt us are the ones forgotten. Because, in such cases, they are driving our way of living without our being aware of it.

The second advantage is that by realizing we are not free in so many unstated ways, we are more apt to take advantage when psychological portals to self-understanding present themselves. In addition, when we fail, as we surely will at times, rather than becoming discouraged, we see more powerfully the need for God's grace and recognize that, while we need to do all we can, we need God's grace even more. This further leads to a greater appreciation of the "communion of saints" not as an anachronistic concept but as a real, necessary reality. Quite simply: *we can't do it alone*. We must be willing to learn again and again not only from our own experiences but also from others who are wiser and holier than we are, about the serious and true Spirit of silence and solitude.

Silence and Solitude

Sara Maitland in *A Book of Silence* shares her unrelenting search for silence. She describes discovery of "bits and pieces of silence woven into the fabric of each day," as well as steps to create them by unplugging a phone or taking a walk where she was least apt to run into someone she knew. Waking earlier than usual also added to the time when silence would be more easily experienced. She also went on to discover that it takes a while before silence becomes a friend you know.

> The experience of most people who voluntarily take themselves off into silence is that it takes a while to settle into it. Of course, it does not grow more silent as time passes, but you do become more attuned to the silence. Unlike sound, which crashes against your ears, silence is subtle. The more and the longer you are silent, the more you hear the tiny noises within the silence, so that silence itself is always slipping away like a timid animal. You have to be very still and lure it. This is hard; one has only to try to quiet one's mind or body to discover just how turbulent they are. But gradually, I discovered a shape for each day and the silence took over.

To silence, Arctic explorer William Byrd would add solitude as having a powerful impact on him—not simply in the moment but for the rest of his life. In his book *Alone* he wrote,

> Aside from the meteorological and auroral work, I had no important purposes. There was nothing of that sort. Nothing whatever, except one man's desire to know that kind of experience to the full, to be by himself for a while and to taste peace and quiet and solitude long enough to find out how good they really are....
>
> I wanted something more than just privacy in the geographical sense. I wanted to sink roots into some replenishing philosophy....
>
> I did take away something that I had not fully possessed before: appreciation of the sheer beauty

> and miracle of being alive, and a humble set of values....Civilization has not altered my ideas. I live more simply now, and with more peace.

Another wonderful experience of spending time in silence and solitude is the ability to experience where the psychological and spiritual veil that is drawn between us and the mystical or heavenly is "thin." The ultimate goal of mindfulness (being in the now with your eyes wide open to life) and prayerfulness (being mindful with an eye to a unitive experience with God) is to allow oneself to be prompted to awe and clarity. We begin to understand more clearly and deeply theoretical physicist, Albert Einstein's, comment that "there are only two ways to live life. One is as though nothing is a miracle. The other is as though everything is."

Eastern spiritual master Shunryu Suzuki notes in his book *Not Always So* that in sitting in meditation, "we [also] actually clear up our various attachments....When I know what I am doing, clearly, without any overestimation or underestimation, very honestly and truly, I do not have much burden on my mind."

Alone-time, in general, offers us a great deal as we make the opportunity for ourselves to notice new life in seeing what we hadn't before in ways that previously weren't possible because of our mindlessness tendencies. One result of this is that we can then make different choices and decisions *if we wish*. In addition, as Ezra Pound would demonstrate later in his life, alone-time led to a "place" where it became possible to listen eloquently, instead of talking eloquently. This "listening" includes questioning ourselves because we are less apt to be concerned—as when we are in public—as to what others would consider socially acceptable in their mirroring our statements and attitudes. Silence and solitude create a milieu in which we are asked: Are we also able to spiritually become awakened to who and what populates our day? Who lives in the cities of our meaning? Will we find that it is primarily only the stony sense of regret?

In times of quiet meditation and contemplation, all of a sudden, we also are in a good position to see certain things we hadn't before and over time broader styles and approaches to life become evident. We begin to recognize and know:

- Being upset points to more than we are crediting as the source of these negative emotions.
- We start to see spontaneous moments not as interruptions but possibilities.
- There is a renewed appreciation of slowing down and a debunking of rushing toward our graves by being involved in projects that the world says are important but sap our very life of its spiritual essence.
- Experiencing each day is not possible when we are enveloped in a cocoon of worry, resentment, anxiety about what may not even happen, preoccupation, and self-consciousness.
- Cancellations sometimes are not fun or may postpone something we want to take care of, but they also do open a space for something new.
- Less time spent on judging and more on becoming intrigued leads to wisdom rather than disappointment.
- Life isn't all about us; people don't wake up in the morning thinking about us. And so, we can realize that so many of our disappointments and causes for discouragement are because of our own egoism.

Quiet Dangers

At the heart of Kyriacos Markides book *Gifts of the Desert* is Father Maximos, whose spiritual roots were planted on Mount Athos, where he spent many years before being asked to be bishop of Cyprus. At one point in the book the author quotes Father as saying, "The saints were not naïve people, you know. They were intelligent and clever human beings, but their cleverness was free of egoism."

When persons undergo tragedy, one potential result is that it uncovers and removes what is false in us and the world. Even when someone close to us dies, we need to release them as they were in life so we can have the space within to remember and live with the love they left us in a new way. Life in its fullest then is not about grasping, egoism, always gaining and holding on to something or someone for security. Instead, it is about the art of releasing at the right time, in the right way, so we can live with the joys of memory in a way that we have room to live differently in the now.

Such a spirit of releasing though takes *humility*, the *acceptance* of change, and a freedom to be *available* to what is happening *now*. You know when you are truly letting go, not by what you are missing but by how much you experience what is fresh and eye-opening. Simplicity and a desire to constantly learn are the cornerstones of a replenishing philosophy and spirituality of life. They offer glimpses of heaven on earth and a child-like (rather than childish) wonder about life, self, meaning, and how we can encounter people, nature, and daily events.

For Reflection...

"Do not be discouraged.
The Holy Spirit is not asleep."

– Thomas Merton to Dan Berrigan

On the other hand, when there is no simplicity present, complexity, conflict, tension, and insecurity reign. We don't need to be on a deserted desert island with palm trees, a little hut, and no responsibilities, but we do need a faith that is willing to face everything and not seek to set up tents of satisfaction for where we are. It is a faith with an openness to let go.

Life can be like one of the challenges on an obstacle course. There is a rope hanging from an overhang. The basic task is to take it, swing over a ditch, and move onto the next task. However, many strong and brave candidates fail. They either swing over and swing back or let go at the last minute and fall into the ditch. The only way to do it is to grab the rope, swing over, and *in mid-air* let go with the faith your feet will land on the other side.

Resistance to Contemplation

Given all that sitting in silence and solitude while wrapped in gratitude can offer us, why is avoidance of contemplation and intimacy with God the norm? And it is. Rabbi Abraham Joshua Heschel attested to this in his book *Who Is Man?*, writing that a person's plight "is not due to the fear of nonbeing, to the fear of death, but to the fear of living." He continues,

> The fear of living arises most commonly out of experiences of failure or insult or having gone astray or having been rebuffed. It is rooted in the encounter with other human beings, in the inability or refusal to communicate, but above all in the failure to live in complete involvement with what transcends our living.

Contemplation initially raises our defensiveness because we recognize our nakedness, which is based on our own sinfulness and seeking to become the god of our own lives. No longer do we walk with a God who planted the tree of knowledge. We seek to do without this gifted relationship and instead seek to walk in the divine garden of life by centering ourselves solely on ourselves. True contemplation unveils this lie and we feel it in different ways.

We recognize that in prayer we are always beginners. In his book *Merton's Palace of Nowhere*, when asked for a way to God in prayer, James Finley used the metaphor of untrodden snow and answered, "Where is the path? The answer is to walk across it and there will be your path." Henri Nouwen in *The Genesee Diary* shared that he always had the fantasy that "one day God just might break through the hard shell of my resistance and reveal himself to me in such an intensive and convincing way that I would be able to let my 'idols' go and commit myself unreservedly to him." To this, his spiritual guide, who was abbot and a psychiatrist, noted that he wasn't surprised by this fantasy and said,

> You want God to appear to you in the way your passions desire, but these passions make you blind to his presence now. Focus on the non-passionate part of yourself and realize God's presence there. Let that part grow in you and make your decisions from there. You will be surprised to see how powers that seem invincible shrink away.

Two other classic resistances are boredom and fear of our shame. Real spirituality dawns when God becomes as real as our life. For this to happen, we need to bring our real concerns to prayer. And, when thoughts arise that are shameful, we can face them *with God*, rather than bury them with a belief: "Oh, well that is just how I am. I wish I could change but have failed again and again." Success is not the goal.

Faithfulness to honesty, humility, and relationship with God is. Also, shame like discouragement is a hidden home of the ego. Kahlil Gibran wrote in his book *Sand and Foam*, "Should we all confess our sins to one another, we would all laugh at our lack of originality."

People also resist time for silence and solitude or have a failure to stop and take a few moments in reflection during different times of the day, because their actions prove they don't think it is worth much. "Where your treasure is, there your heart will be also," Jesus said (Matt 6:21; Luke 12:34). When we recognize that prayer is the heart of life, then the rest of life changes. If we feel it is a nice add-on, then little happens in us.

More resistances to being alone with God—as opposed to merely alone with our own ego—are of course present and books on meditation and contemplation expand on them. (See "Themes Worth Pursuing Further" at the end of the book for reading recommendations.) However, it is solely the purpose of this chapter to help us to recognize that we all resist prayer. Knowing that is not a prompt for discouragement or disagreement. It is simply the stage on which to begin to uncover our resistances when they show up, increase our awareness to what moments in prayer do to enliven our day and life, and become faithful in looking for the crumbs of spiritual mindfulness in our lives that are already there. As Erling Kagge wrote in his book *Silence in the Age of Noise*, "Life is long, if we listen to ourselves often enough, and look up."

Rachel Corbett in her book *You Must Change Your Life* wrote about Rainer Maria Rilke and Auguste Rodin. She remarked that Rilke at one point in his life "felt like he was failing a test he shouldn't have been taking in the first place." Understanding and making friends with the resistances to prayer and new awareness, allows us to uncover such events in our own lives so we can truly become more alive and embrace the living God, rather than simply go permanently astray, moving from one task to another, interrupted only by boredom, exhaustion, and occasional pleasant distractions of existence.

The choice is up to us. Will we take the road less traveled and make the best choice? The response to that question is not made once and for all but *each* day of our lives in quiet prayer, marked by a spirit of intrigue and love if we truly give priority to such moments. As Thomas Merton notes, "In silence, God ceases to be an object and becomes an experience." The question is: Do we truly want that to happen, or will we spend the remainder of our lives merely wistfully thinking or talking about it?

Epilogue

Anomie?

Our gods have to die before we reach for the God who is beyond all our human images and projections and who waits over the brink of the known in darkness.

– Constance FitzGerald
The Desire for God and the Transformative Power of Contemplation

Each time we consent to a new light on our weakness and powerlessness, we are in a deeper place with Christ.

– Thomas Keating

A patient came in to see me for the first time. I motioned him to sit in the chair opposite me. In response, he first sat down and then using both hands on the arms of the chair lifted himself in the air, leaving his wooden clogs on the floor while simultaneously crossing his legs under him as he sat back down. When I asked him how I could be of help, he said, "I am suffering from *anomie*."

Émile Durkheim, founder of modern sociology, described *anomie* as a psychological sense of worthlessness, frustration, a lack of purpose, and despair. Although I had heard the term used before in one of my undergraduate texts. In response, I said as I would have if he said he was anxious, under stress, or depressed, "Why don't you describe when it began and how you have responded to it?"

When he told his story, it became evident that he was a very sensitive person who experienced life uniquely and intently but that for a while such experiences were not rewarding but disorienting. The individual sounds in his psychological orchestra were blaring, so he was unable to enjoy the meaningful overall symphony of his life. It had become simultaneously "too much" and "not enough." He was lost.

Today, with COVID-19 and other crises, many feel they have lost their way. The media doesn't have to exaggerate or focus on the negative to overwhelm us with natural disasters, political upheaval, divisiveness, and modern medical challenges that never seem to end. Persons thrown off their normal schedule find themselves multitasking or bored, alone, and encompassed by periods of silence and solitude for which they are ill-prepared. They have gone from mindlessness to emptiness because they don't know how to be mindful, prayerful.

With the patient I just mentioned, I responded to his expression of *anomie* with a journey to find new meaning and to use his sensitivity to open himself up to appreciate portals in purpose that he didn't know were there or how to open them. In today's society, the same call is now present for all of us. Many will go down the psychological and spiritual dead ends of projection, anger, and blame, or guilt and discouragement. However, today's disorientation can also open the door to intrigue about how they may live their lives going forward moment by moment: with a new set of greater values; appreciation—rather than denial—of personal vulnerability; understanding of true friendship; and an appreciation of how being compassionate is a circle of grace that helps us even when we are in the darkness. As a result, our relationship with Someone or Something greater than us can become deeper than ever before. A more beautiful psychological and spiritual symphony is possible when we entertain such a possibility and look for it with hope and some guidance.

Sometimes brief stories decide to steadfastly remain in your memory. There may be a lot of other experiences of the past that are larger, more imperative, and formative...but certain events still remain close to the surface, undaunted, and unapologetic. They are there and their message seems to be: "Live with it."

For me, one of them is a brief story told by Anthony DeMello in his book *One Minute Wisdom* that I dearly loved because of its simplicity and power. In it, a person boards a boat to cross a river to a revered and famous temple. As they push off the shore, he asks the boatman if he has ever visited the temple. In response, the man replies, "No, because I haven't fully fathomed the beauty of this river."

Without meaning to, life has carried me among the famous. I was at a news conference for the Beatles, a party attended by the Beach Boys and the Smothers Brothers, and I spoke on Capitol Hill. Yet, the strange thing for me is that in interacting with stars, as well as noted therapists, gurus, and other accomplished human beings, I found they often didn't seem to enjoy the moment they were in. They were not able to be an encouraging model and presence to others so they could fathom their own present moments while looking to the future with hope and compassion.

Then, I would meet unknown persons of peace and joy. Almost without my knowing it, they would invite me into an orbit that was so, so interested in me enjoying and enriching *my* moment. When this occurred, I found that it enabled me, in turn, to also help others to find the serenity and fun they sought. I began to realize that understanding and facing *anomie* is truly contagious when you are with the right "characters of

God" and seek what they seek and have already found in many ways.

It was a radical journey in simple steps and occasional leaps. Settling was out. There was too little time in life for that. And, through it all, the words of one of the Abbas (Fathers) of the fourth century repeatedly returned me to the path I wanted to follow when I would fall off it again and again. Those simple powerful words were: *Seek God and not where God lives.*

To do this we must value a real sense of spiritual intimacy in which we do not have "psychological rooms hidden from God." There must be a commitment to having a relationship with the truth that becomes more enticing than the inflation and protection of our own fragile ego. That is what *Hidden Dangers* has been about. It was meant to be a "voice" to encourage the journey to integrate autonomy, our will, with theonomy, God's will, so we can more fully, each day, enjoy the life we have been given and be truly compassionate, without expecting anything in return.

Now, that you have read this brief work to prime the psychological pump, to center yourself and move forward, it is now your turn to take the next steps. Only you can do it—given your own personality and history. Only you can do it—with the sense of passion and commitment you can muster. Your answer can be to settle, to become defensive when anything in this book has touched a spiritual sore point or to decide to humbly open the psychological doors in an effort to hide nothing from God...and from yourself.

In the process of these efforts, you will fail *again* and *again* for as Jesus says in Matthew 7:14, "But small is the gate and narrow the road that leads to life, and only a few ever find it." That is why St. Benedict reminded his own brothers, "Always we begin again." Certainly, if there is a spiritual "key" to the gate, supported by a psychological one, it is *humility*.

And so, as I firmly believe and have repeatedly stated:

Epilogue: *Anomie?*

When you take knowledge and you add humility, you get wisdom.

Then, when you take this very wisdom and add it to compassion, you get love.

And such pure love is at the heart of a rich, well lived life because...*God is love.*

Works Cited

Prologue: Quiet Dangers

Heschel, Abraham Joshua. *God in Search of Man*

Norris, Kathleen. *Dakota*

Sosetti-Ferencei, Jennifer. *On Being and Becoming*

Introduction: Rooms Hidden from God

DeMello, Anthony. *One Minute Wisdom*

Heschel, Abraham Joshua. *God in Search of Man*

Leech, Kenneth. *True Prayer*

Matthew, Iain. *Impact of God*

Merton, Thomas. *New Seeds of Contemplation*

Merton, Thomas. *Wisdom of the Desert*

Rilke, Rainer Maria. *Letters to a Young Poet*

Gosetti-Ferencei, Jennifer. *On Being and Becoming*

1. "Do You Want to Be Made Whole?"

Buber, Martin. *Way of Man*

Heschel, Abraham Joshua. *God in Search of Man*

Heschel, Abraham Joshua. *The Insecurity of Freedom*

Heschel, Abraham Joshua. *Who Is Man?*

Heschel, Abraham Joshua. *The Wisdom of Heschel* (Edited by Ruth Marcus)

Lama, Dalai, and Desmond Tutu. *The Book of Joy*

McCloskey, Pat. *Naming Your God: The Search for Mature Images*

Palmer, Parker. *Let Your Life Speak*

Platt, Sylvia, and Ted Hughes. *The Silent Woman*

Suzuki, Shunryu. *Not Always So*

Whitman, Walt. *Song of Myself*

Wicks, Robert J. *Touching the Holy*

2. The Exhilarating Psychological Search for *Imago Dei*

Csikszentmihalyi, Mihaly. *Flow*

Madigan, Stephen. *Narrative Therapy*

Palmer, Parker. *Let Your Life Speak*

Peterson, Christopher. *A Primer on Positive Psychology*

Seligman, Martin. *Authentic Happiness*

White, Michael, and David Epston. *Narrative Means to Therapeutic Ends*

Wicks, Robert J. *Perspective: The Calm within the Storm*

3. Traveling Your Own Road to Emmaus

DeMello, Anthony. *One Minute Wisdom*

Frankl, Viktor. *Man's Search for Inner Meaning*

Hitz, Zena. *Lost in Thought*

Kagge, Erling. *Silence in an Age of Noise*

Peterson, Eugene. *Practice Resurrection: A Conversation on Growing Up in Christ*

Shuzuki, Shunryu, in David Chadwick. *The Crooked Cucumber*

Werdel, Mary Beth, and Robert J. Wicks. *A Primer on Posttraumatic Growth*

4. Overcoming Psychological Resistance to Spiritual Wisdom

Byrd, Richard. *Alone*

Corbett, Rachel. *You Must Change Your Life*

Crane, George. *Bones of the Master*

Farnham, Suzanne, Joseph Gill, R. Taylor McLean, and Susan Word. *Listening Hearts*

Gibran, Kahlil. *Sand and Foam*

Kagge, Erling. *Silence in an Age of Noise*

Maitland, Sara. *A Book of Silence*

Markides, Kyriacos. *Gifts of the Desert*

Penny, Louise. *All the Devils Are Here: A Novel*

Sanford, John. *Healing and Wholeness*

Smoley, Richard. *Inner Christianity*

Wicks, Robert J. *Seeds of Sensitivity*

Wicks, Robert J. *Simple Changes*

Epilogue: *Anomie?*

FitzGerald, OCD, Constance. "The Desire for God and the Transformative Power of Contemplation," in Mary Heather MacKinnon, Moni McIntyre, and Mary Ellen Sheehan, eds., *Light Burdens, Heavy Blessings: Challenges of Church and Culture in a Post Vatican II Era*

Themes Worth Pursuing Further

~ Books to Consider ~

The following works are from psychology and spirituality, as well as from different world religions, as a way to enhance and deepen the search for spiritual wisdom.

Simplicity and Ordinariness

Bode, Richard. *First You Have to Row a Little Boat*

Georgiou, S. T. *The Way of the Dreamcatcher*

Hoff, Benjamin. *The Te of Piglet*

Palmer, Parker. *Let Your Life Speak*

Wicks, Robert J. *The Tao of Ordinariness*

Silence and Solitude

Byrd, Richard. *Alone*

Maitland, Sara. *A Book of Silence*

Merton, Thomas. *New Seeds of Contemplation*

Merton, Thomas. *Wisdom of the Desert*

Nouwen, Henri. *Way of the Heart*

Storr, Anthony. *Solitude: A Return to Self*

Overcoming Psychological Resistance to Change

Wicks, Robert J. *Simple Changes*

Freud, Anna. *Ego and the Mechanisms of Defense*

The Search for Spiritual Wisdom

Brazier, David. *Zen Therapy*

DeMello, Anthony. *One Minute Wisdom*

France, Peter. *A Place of Healing for the Soul: Patmos*

Harvey, Andrew. *Journey in Ladakh*

Heschel, Abraham. *God in Search of Man*

Johnson, Sandy. *The Book of Tibetan Elders*

Lama, Dalai, and Desmond Tutu with Douglas Abrams. *The Book of Joy*

Markides, Kyriacos. *Gifts of the Desert*

Nouwen, Henri. *Making All Things New*

Ricard, Matthieu. *Happiness*

Rilke, Rainer Maria. *Letters to a Young Poet*

Compassion

Nouwen, Henri, Donald McNeil, and Douglas Morrison. *Compassion*

Wicks, Robert J. *Night Call: Embracing Compassion and Hope in a Troubled World*

Gaining, Regaining, and Maintaining a Healthy Perspective

Wicks, Robert J. *Perspective: The Calm within the Storm*

Resilience and Posttraumatic Growth

Frankl, Viktor. *Man's Search for Inner Meaning*

Joseph, Stephen. *What Doesn't Kill Us: The New Psychology of Posttraumatic Growth*

Werdel, Mary Beth, and Robert J. Wicks. *A Primer on Posttraumatic Growth*

Wicks, Robert J. *Bounce: Living the Resilient Life*

Wicks, Robert J. *Riding the Dragon*

Wicks, Robert J. *The Simple Care of a Hopeful Heart*

Spiritual Darkness

Cassidy, Laurie, and M. Shawn Copeland (eds.). *Desire, Darkness, and Hope: Theology in a Time of Impasse—Engaging the Thought of Constance FitzGerald, OCD*

Mathew, Iain. *Impact of God*

Prayer

Steindl-Rast, David. *Gratefulness, the Heart of Prayer*

Wicks, Robert J. *Prayerfulness*

Wicks, Robert J. (ed.). *Prayer in the Catholic Tradition*

Biographies of Spiritual Figures

Chadwick, David. *The Crooked Cucumber: The Life and Zen Teaching of Shunryu Suzuki*

duBoulay, Shirley. *Beyond the Darkness: A Biography of Bede Griffiths*

Iyer, Pico. *The Open Road: The Global Journey of the Fourteenth Dalai Lama*

McGregor, Michael N. *Pure Act: The Uncommon Life of Robert Lax*

Telushkin, Joseph. *Rebbe*

Existentialism

Bakewell, Sarah. *At the Existentialist Café*

About the Author

For over thirty-five years, **Dr. Robert Wicks** has been called upon to speak calm into chaos by individuals and groups experiencing great stress, anxiety, and confusion.

Dr. Wicks received his doctorate in psychology (PsyD) from Hahnemann Medical College and Hospital, is professor emeritus at Loyola University Maryland, and has taught in universities and professional schools of psychology, medicine, nursing, theology, education, counseling, and social work. He was also the commencement speaker for Wright State School of Medicine and Stritch School of Medicine, as well as the commencement speaker for, and the recipient of honorary doctorates from Georgian Court, Caldwell, and Marywood Universities.

In addition, in the past Dr. Wicks has spoken on his major areas of expertise—resilience, self-care, the prevention of *secondary* stress (pressures encountered in reaching out to others), and the integration of psychology with classic spiritual wisdom—on Capitol Hill to members of Congress and their chiefs of staff, at Johns Hopkins School of Medicine, the U.S. Air Force Academy, the Mayo Clinic, the North American Aerospace Defense Command, the Defense Intelligence Agency, as well as at Boston's Children's Hospital, Harvard Divinity School, Yale School of Nursing, Princeton Theological Seminary, and to members of the NATO Intelligence Fusion Center in England. He spoke at the Boston Public Library's commemoration of the Boston Marathon bombing, addressed 10,000 educators in the Air Canada Arena in Toronto, was the opening keynote speaker to 1,500 physicians for the American

Medical Directors Association; has spoken at the FBI and New York City Police Academies; led a course on resilience in Beirut for relief workers from Aleppo, Syria; and addressed caregivers in twenty countries, including China, Vietnam, India, Thailand, Haiti, Northern Ireland, Hungary, Guatemala, Malta, New Zealand, Australia, France, England, and South Africa.

Dr. Wicks was responsible for the psychological debriefing for relief workers with NGOs who were evacuated from Rwanda during the genocide, and he worked in Cambodia with professionals from the English-speaking community who were present to help the Khmer people rebuild their nation following years of terror and torture. He delivered presentations on self-care at the National Naval Medical Center in Bethesda Maryland and Walter Reed Army Hospital to health care professionals responsible for Iraq and Afghan war veterans. More recently, Dr. Wicks addressed U.S. Army health care professionals returning from Africa, where they were assisting during the Ebola crisis, and he spoke virtually during the COVID-19 pandemic on resilience and self-care to thousands of physicians, nurses, and educators.

Dr. Wicks has published more than fifty books for both professionals and the general public. His spirituality books include *Riding the Dragon*, *Heartstorming: Creating a Place God Can Call Home*, and *Prayers for Uncertain Times*. Among his latest books from Oxford University Press are *The Simple Care of a Hopeful Heart*, *The Tao of Ordinariness*, *Perspective*, and *Bounce: Living the Resilient Life*. His books for professionals include works for physicians, nurses, psychologists, and persons in ministry. He is the recipient of the first annual Alumni Award for Excellence in Professional Psychology from Widener University, the Humanitarian of the Year Award from the American Counseling Association's Division on Spirituality, Ethics and Religious Values in Counseling, and the papal medal, *Pro Ecclesia et Pontifice*.

Also by Robert J. Wicks from Paulist Press

***"Do You Have a Moment?"** 50 Spiritual Posts to Open and Close the Day* offers a glimpse of lived spirituality from the author's perspective as he has encountered the circle of God's grace in his own life and shared it with others on the way…for a moment, here and there.

"This is one of those rare little books that delivers what it promises, insights that open awareness to the realization of peace, gratitude, love, and joy. It's a delight to read just one reflection a day because the writing is so good, you linger on sentences."

– Michael Leach, author of *Soul Seeing*

"'Spiritual' books so often read 'thin.' But here are grounded insights born in and for tough times that breathe in with the halting rhythm of a tired heart and out with the grateful release of soul-care."

– Wendy M. Wright, professor emerita of theology, Creighton University

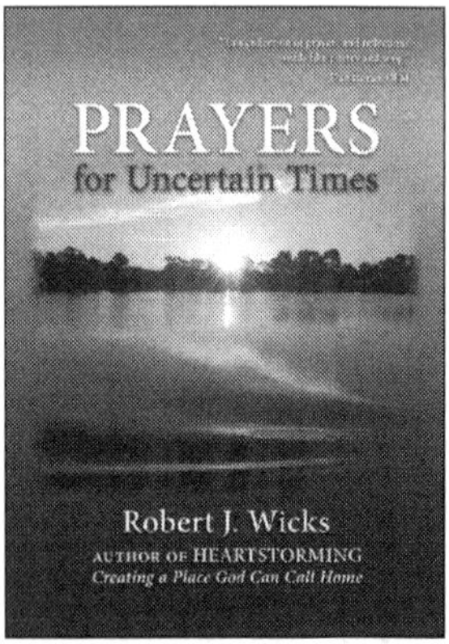

Prayers for Uncertain Times includes selected and new prayers, reflections, and dialogues all under one cover in a brief work that is easy to carry along during the day. With the conviction that a creative use of imagery allows us to surface a sense of God and self in a vivid and personally compelling way, Wicks also offers readers a straightforward process to write from their spiritual experiences and thereby embrace holiness in prayer and action.

He says, "When we pray and ask God to find us again in surprising ways amidst the darkness, the portal to a transformed Divine relationship is seen in new ways under different circumstances. And, accordingly, how we live our life going forward is made new. *All things are made new*. With true prayer, nothing less than this should be sought and much more than this is possible." Author Robert Wicks desires through *Prayers for Uncertain Times* to offer hope, encouragement, and direction in the uncertain times in which we live.

Heartstorming was awarded both first place among spirituality books for excellence in publishing by the Association of Catholic Publishers, and a commendation from the Catholic Media Association in its contemporary spirituality book awards in 2021.

Heartstorming: *Creating a Place God Can Call Home* provides a point of entry to the contemplative life for anyone who will become or remain open to the movements of God in their daily life. The author's forty-five field notes show what can result if the reader takes a journey of growth in being spiritually directed and then goes on to write field notes by using the simple process Wicks makes available.

Through his own experience of God's nearness and drawing from his deep understanding of the human condition, Robert Wicks puts within reach of us all a healthy spiritual perspective as part of everyday living. Dr. Wicks writes convincingly and in practical terms, giving guidance to both the spiritually adventurous and weary souls among us. In all, he emphasizes the importance of listening to the inner life—mind, will, and emotions—on our way to an increasingly fresh engagement with God's will and purposes in and around us.

Related Books by Robert J. Wicks

The Simple Care of a Hopeful Heart: Mentoring Yourself in Difficult Times

Do You Have a Moment?: 50 Spiritual Posts to Open and Close the Day

Night Call: Embracing Compassion and Hope in a Troubled World

The Tao of Ordinariness: Humility and Simplicity in a Narcissistic Age

Perspective: The Calm within the Storm

Bounce: Living the Resilient Life

Prayers for Uncertain Times

Heartstorming: Creating a Place God Can Call Home

Living a Gentle, Passionate Life

After 50: Spiritually Embracing Your Own Wisdom Years

Handbook of Spirituality for Ministers, Vols. I and II (editor)

Clinical Handbook of Pastoral Counseling, Vols. I–III (senior co-editor)

Prayer in the Catholic Tradition: A Handbook of Practical Approaches (editor)

Conversations with a Guardian Angel: A Novel

No Problem: Turning the Next Corner in the Spiritual Life

Availability: The Problem and the Gift

Prayerfulness: Awakening to the Fullness of Life

Everyday Simplicity: A Practical Guide to Spiritual Growth

Riding the Dragon: 10 Lessons for Inner Strength in Challenging Times

Touching the Holy: Ordinariness, Self-Esteem, and Friendship

Simple Changes: Quietly Overcoming Barriers to Personal and Professional Growth

The Resilient Clinician

The Inner Life of the Counselor

A Primer on Posttraumatic Growth: An Introduction and Guide (co-author)

Clinician's Guide to Self-Renewal: Essential Advice from the Field (senior co-editor)